Inside Copilot

Inside Copilot is designed to teach users to master Copilot, Microsoft's generative AI assistant. Learn prompt engineering and use cases for Copilot in many Microsoft products at beginner, intermediate, and expert levels. Perfect for any professionals who find their schedules packed with repetitive computer tasks, Copilot can automatically generate PowerPoint presentations, draft emails on Outlook, write code on GitHub, and more. Both companies and individuals can learn to utilize Copilot to significantly speed up processes and gain an advantage.

More information about this series at `https://link.springer.com/bookseries/17432`.

Your New Colleague is a Copilot

Aligning Technology, Talent, and Trust

Jared Matfess

Apress®

Your New Colleague is a Copilot: Aligning Technology, Talent, and Trust

Jared Matfess
Berlin, CT, USA

ISBN-13 (pbk): 979-8-8688-2618-4
ISBN-13 (electronic): 979-8-8688-2619-1
https://doi.org/10.1007/979-8-8688-2619-1

Managing Director, Apress Media LLC: Welmoed Spahr
Acquisitions Editor: Ryan Byrnes
Coordinating Editor: Gryffin Winkler

Cover image by eStudioCalamar

Distributed to the book trade worldwide by Springer Science+Business Media New York, 1 New York Plaza, New York, NY 10004. Phone 1-800-SPRINGER, fax (201) 348-4505, e-mail orders-ny@springer-sbm.com, or visit www.springeronline.com. Apress Media, LLC is a Delaware LLC and the sole member (owner) is Springer Science + Business Media Finance Inc (SSBM Finance Inc). SSBM Finance Inc is a **Delaware** corporation.

For information on translations, please e-mail booktranslations@springernature.com; for reprint, paperback, or audio rights, please e-mail bookpermissions@springernature.com.

Apress titles may be purchased in bulk for academic, corporate, or promotional use. eBook versions and licenses are also available for most titles. For more information, reference our Print and eBook Bulk Sales web page at http://www.apress.com/bulk-sales.

Any source code or other supplementary material referenced by the author in this book is available to readers on GitHub (https://github.com/Apress). For more detailed information, please visit https://www.apress.com/gp/services/source-code.

If disposing of this product, please recycle the paper

To the late Professor John Gray at the University of Hartford.

You were plain-spoken, a little gruff, and always wore a smirk that let us know you were in on the joke. You taught us the syntax of Perl and the basics of web design, but you left us with something far more durable. You taught us that the purpose of education isn't to walk away having all the answers; it is to master the ability to learn. In a world changing as fast as this one, that lesson has meant everything.

And to the next generation of builders.

I know where you are because I used to be you. I grew up sitting on the floor in the back corner of a Borders, trying to stay out of sight of the employees, devouring books on Macromedia Flash, HTML, and C#. I couldn't afford the fifty-dollar price tags, so I sat there for hours, "stealing" knowledge page by page. For me, those aisles were an escape from the mundane and a doorway into a world where I could create anything I could imagine. I owe my entire career to the authors who wrote those books.

I hope this book helps you build what comes next.

Table of Contents

About the Author

Jared Matfess is a solutions architect at AvePoint, specializing in helping organizations maximize the value of their investments in Microsoft technologies. He is a co-author of *Microsoft 365 Copilot at Work: Using AI to Get the Most from Your Business Data and Favorite Apps* (John Wiley & Sons, Inc., 2024) and author of *Microsoft Copilot Studio Quick Start: Learn to Create and Deploy Personalized AI Solutions* (John Wiley & Sons, Inc., 2025). Jared holds certifications from both Microsoft and AWS and was recognized seven times as a Microsoft MVP in the Office Apps & Services, and Copilot categories from 2016 to 2022. He earned a bachelor's degree in Interactive Information Technology from the University of Hartford, an MBA from the University of Massachusetts Amherst, and a master's degree in Computer Information Systems from Boston University.

About the Technical Reviewer

Zewei Song is a developer, support engineer, consultant, and architect based in the Chicagoland area. He holds a PhD in control engineering and possesses multiple professional certifications, including Certified ScrumMaster, Microsoft Certified Master for SharePoint, Trainer, and Cybersecurity Architect Expert, among others.

Zewei has extensive experience in consulting, proactive support, and technical advisory. He spent nearly 17 years at Microsoft as a senior consultant and field engineer before joining Discover Financial Services as Senior Manager, overseeing the Microsoft 365 portfolio. Zewei later became a Cloud Solution Architect at Invoke, LLC, an award-winning Microsoft partner, where he contributed to building its consulting practice focused on Microsoft 365 and Copilot.

In early 2026, Zewei rejoined Microsoft as a Senior Cloud Solution Architect – AI Business Solutions within its Global Customer Success (GCS) organization, where he focuses on advancing Copilot adoption and leading AI-driven transformation initiatives.

Zewei's professional goal is to lead and inspire organizations to get the most out of their technology investments while boosting productivity for end users. Outside of work, he enjoys a happy family life with his wife Ying and two children, Albert and Emily, and spends his free time bicycling and doing photography.

Acknowledgments

Books usually don't happen by accident, but this one almost did.

To **Ryan Byrnes**, who approached me at the AI World Tour in New York City: I was already midway through writing a book on Copilot Studio. I still can't believe you convinced me that writing *another* book simultaneously was a rational decision. Thank you for the push, the patience, and for seeing the vision before I did.

This work is the culmination of 11 years at a Fortune 50 manufacturer, a decade in consulting, and my current role at AvePoint. It is built on the reality of how business and technology actually collide.

A huge thank-you to the people who helped shape that reality:

- **Deepak Gandhi** at Visa, for the shared stories and the constant encouragement.
- **Norm Young** at AvePoint, for the unwavering support and for refusing to let me stop writing, even when the schedule got crazy.
- **Heidi Lamar**, my early peer editor. Thank you for teaching me to focus on the people side of the equation. If this book feels human, it is because of you.

Finally, to the context in which this was written. This manuscript wasn't crafted in a quiet study. It was hammered out on planes, trains, and in the back of automobiles. It spans a whirlwind year of 80+ flights, 70 nights in hotel rooms, and hundreds of hours of client conversations.

This book was born in motion. Thank you to everyone who helped keep it moving.

Introduction

AI is here. It's not a sci-fi prediction; it's your new virtual coworker.

Tools like Copilot and ChatGPT have already reshaped the landscape. The debate on "whether to adopt" is over. Now, the race is on to do it right—responsibly, repeatedly, and for real results.

I've spent years working with organizations trying to figure this out. I've seen the failures: the endless pilot cycles, the reckless deployments, and the tech-first approaches that forgot about the humans. But the patterns for success are just as clear. The winners invest in trust. They build systems that scale. They make AI something people *want* to use, rather than something that is done *to* them.

This book is for the leaders, managers, and builders who want to replicate that success. If you're tired of scattered priorities and unclear expectations, you're in the right place.

We're going to use a framework called **IGNITE**. It's your road map to scaling AI without the chaos:

- **Inspire** people to care, reducing fear and sparking curiosity.
- **Gauge** your readiness so you know your data and risk posture.
- **Nail** the pilots that have a realistic chance of success.
- **Iterate** the models and prompts with deliberate focus.
- **Track** the impact in a way leadership actually trusts.

- **Embed** governance that guides you rather than blocks you.
- **Scale** the capability across the enterprise.

This isn't a rigid textbook. It's a tool kit. You'll find real stories, practical exercises, and strategies you can apply immediately.

Potential is great, but execution is everything. By the end of this book, you'll have the blueprint to introduce AI intentionally, manage the human side of change, and guide your organization through the next evolution of work.

Let's begin.

CHAPTER 1

GenAI in the Workplace

We are the spark that will light the fire, that will burn the First Order down.

—*Star Wars: The Last Jedi*

The Spark

I grew up completely fascinated by technology ever since my father brought home an IBM PS/2 386 and set it up in our basement. I have been fascinated with computers ever since my father brought home an IBM PS/2 Model 30 286 from his work. It was the late 1980s, and personal computers were not commonplace just yet. Outside of trips to the local Radio Shack, this was the first time I had been up close with a computer. I watched my father navigate between DOS and his Lotus 1-2-3 application and tried to memorize the commands.

I mostly looked over his shoulder until one afternoon when he said he had a surprise for me. He popped in a 3.5" floppy disk that wasn't his usual Lotus 1-2-3 account software and booted into a screen that showed off

J. Matfess, *Your New Colleague is a Copilot*, Inside Copilot,
https://doi.org/10.1007/979-8-8688-2619-1_1

colors with the classic 8-bit audio that would define my childhood. King's Quest I was the spark that ignited my love for computers and ultimately changed the trajectory of my life.

That enthusiasm and love for technology have continued to follow me throughout my career. I helped design and build a campus-wide wireless network, oversaw the rollout of Windows XP, built Intranets, migrated from Lotus Notes to Microsoft 365, and built a technology consulting practice. It's incredible to me how that initial spark that I had when I was young has been able to carry me so long, both personally and professionally. Over time, that flame has died down a bit, but recently, I have felt that same familiar mix of excitement and curiosity with the recent boom of Generative AI ("GenAI").

AI Is the New Spark

AI is coming to all aspects of work, whether an organization is completely bought in or not. Almost every single Independent Software Vendor (ISV) has or is working on integrating AI into some aspect of their product offerings. Microsoft has integrated GenAI into its popular Microsoft 365 SaaS offering with its Copilot offering. Google has taken its Gemini model and made it available in its Google Workspace platform. Adobe is working on creating models that can generate photo-realistic images. So, while you might not be ready to build your own custom AI-powered applications, you should know that many of the software vendors that you currently subscribe to are looking to bring these capabilities to you.

While the marketing is oftentimes outpacing the actual capabilities that companies are bringing to market, the hype is still somewhat real. Much like other business process automation technologies such as Macros, workflows, and robotics process automation ("RPA"), there are productivity gains to be realized through automation. Therefore, the reality is it's not a matter of "if you'll adopt AI"; it's really "when will you choose to adopt AI." And when it comes to AI, one of the most exciting variations, of course, is Generative AI.

GenAI "in Plain English"

One of the most important challenges for introducing AI into your organization is helping to frame up what it is and, in some instances, what it isn't. AI isn't exactly a new technology concept; it's been around for many decades now. However, for many, it hasn't been very approachable, as to be a practitioner required a heavy data science background. GenAI, however, puts natural language at the center of every user interaction. By turning conversation into the control surface for software, tools like ChatGPT make advanced capabilities available to anyone and are reshaping how people work, learn, and create.

A helpful framing for your talk track is recognizing that over the last four decades, we have seen computing move from monochrome terminals to graphical desktops, then to a global internet and always-on mobile devices. Each of these major innovations has unlocked new ways of working, collaborating, and building new solutions. GenAI is the next major inflection point because it removes the need for commands, code, or navigation.

GenAI excels at turning a blank page into a first draft and a pile of documents into a concise brief. It can spin up blog posts, user stories, or code snippets in seconds, letting creators focus on refinement rather than staring at an empty cursor. The same models can analyze lengthy reports, emails, or meeting transcripts and surface the key points, action items, and risks that matter most. By automating both creation and summarization, GenAI compresses research cycles, speeds decision-making, and frees people to spend more time on insight and strategy.

At a high level, GenAI fundamentally performs two actions:

- **Content Creation** - Based on the prompt that you send, the technology behind the scenes will create new content such as articles, blog posts, social media copy, PowerPoint slides, etc.
- **Content Summarization** - GenAI can review an existing document or dataset and provide insights on the document, such as what it "believes" are the most salient points, the projected reading level of the content, etc. Since it's trained on language, it can even provide suggestions for subjective points such as tone and clarity.

Note Artificial intelligence is the broad field of systems that sense, reason, and act. GenAI is a specialized branch that learns patterns in data to produce new content such as text, code, or images.

Key Technical Concept: Large Language Models

There are a couple of core concepts that are helpful to understand as they pertain to GenAI that will help you in your journey with driving adoption within your organization. The first is understanding that the "brains" behind GenAI are Large Language Models ("LLMs"). LLMs are advanced systems that are trained to understand and generate humanlike text. This training involves analyzing massive amounts of written data including books, websites, and research documents. At a high level, training an LLM follows these steps:

1. **Data Preparation** - Finding and cleaning data that you will use to train your model.
2. **Tokenization** - Breaking the data up into chunks such as words or sub-words.
3. **Vectorization** - Converting tokens into vectors (numerical representations) that the models can ingest and process.
4. **Model Training** - The model learns by predicting the next token in a sequence. For example, providing reinforcement that if it sees the text "Mary had a," the most likely sequence of text to follow would be "little lamb."

While many think that GenAI is some sort of magic, the reality is much more logical. GenAI is just very good at understanding language and then predicting the desired next sequence of words to satisfy your answer. For example, when you prompt ChatGPT "What barnyard animal did Mary have in the popular children's rhyme," it believes with a high degree of certainty that "lamb" is the correct sequence of characters in that string. This is, of course, an oversimplification of what has taken decades of computer and data scientists to develop. However, having a high-level understanding of how GenAI works is important as you work to introduce this to individuals within your organization.

Note A prompt is the text or other input that you provide to an LLM to tell it what you want. Your prompt sets the context and guides the model's response.

Extending GenAI to Your Business's Data

Now, if your experience with GenAI is mostly using ChatGPT, Copilot, or one of the many other consumer-facing services, you might be quick to point out that these services lack domain-specific knowledge about your company. If you recall, the way these LLMs work is that they are trained on large amounts of data. Therefore, if you think about it, the business context that you are most likely looking for would not be generally available for training public LLMs. Your first thought may perhaps be that it would make sense to build your own LLM with company-specific data. However, this can be a costly exercise as creating your own LLM consists of

- **Compute Costs** – The biggest expense, covering high-performing graphical processing units (GPUs), likely by a company such as Nvidia. For reference, GPT-4 reportedly costs over $80 million to perform the necessary training.
- **Data Acquisition** – This includes a mix of IT resource and human resource costs to obtain, cleanse, and format for AI model training.
- **Cloud Infrastructure** – Most organizations would not have the on-premises resources necessary to facilitate training; therefore, they would rely on cloud providers like AWS, Google Cloud, or Microsoft Azure for compute, storage, and networking.
- **Human Expertise** – AI researchers, engineers, and data scientists contribute to model development, fine-tuning, and optimization, adding to labor costs.
- **Operational and Maintenance Costs** – Running and improving models post-training requires ongoing expenses, including hosting and scaling to meet demand.

As you can imagine, cost will be a barrier for most organizations outside the cloud providers developing their own custom AI models. However, the value in AI isn't in being able to provide you with baking recipes or data jokes; it's about helping businesses work more efficiently and create better customer experiences. There are a couple of technical approaches to helping GenAI leverage your enterprise data despite not being trained on it. Each approach includes its own set of work, both technical and business, to help orchestrate.

This book isn't meant to turn you into a data scientist or teach you how to build AI apps from scratch. But to support change management as your organization adopts this technology, you do need a baseline understanding—because there will be tasks that land on your plate.

IGNITE: A Framework for Introducing GenAI to Your Organization

Over the course of my career, I have helped dozens of organizations transform the way that they work. Through these initiatives, I have gained exposure to various project and change management frameworks that are meant to help ensure that the organizations realize their desired outcomes. These frameworks also help to introduce a certain level of repeatability to reduce the amount of time that you are spending recreating the proverbial wheel. They also allow you to help gauge where you are from a project timeline perspective. However, unlike smaller initiatives such as upgrading a network switch or changing a benefits carrier, introducing AI into your organization is transformational. It has the potential to disrupt multiple facets of not only how people complete tasks but how they even think about their work.

As much as AI is a transformation, the core components of introducing it to your organization are like any other large organizational transformation. I have also been fortunate to have helped multiple organizations with their AI-driven transformations at all stages. And when I take a step back, regardless of the organization, the technology platform, or the use cases, I have found some similarities exist. I am not a certified change-management practitioner, but I have seen what works on the ground. Therefore, I want to package up those lessons learned and share them with you, the reader, to help you accelerate your own AI initiatives. This set of steps that I've observed many AI-transformation projects follow is what we will refer to here on out as IGNITE.

IGNITE lays out six practical checkpoints—Inspire, Gauge, Nail, Iterate, Track, and Embed. This IGNITE wheel, as pictured in Figure 1-1, is representative of the process that organizations follow to move an idea from proof-of-concept to business habit. We will leverage this framework throughout the book to guide you through your AI transformation initiatives. Over the next few pages, we'll go through a quick overview of each of these steps in the IGNITE framework and then explore them further in the subsequent chapters of this book.

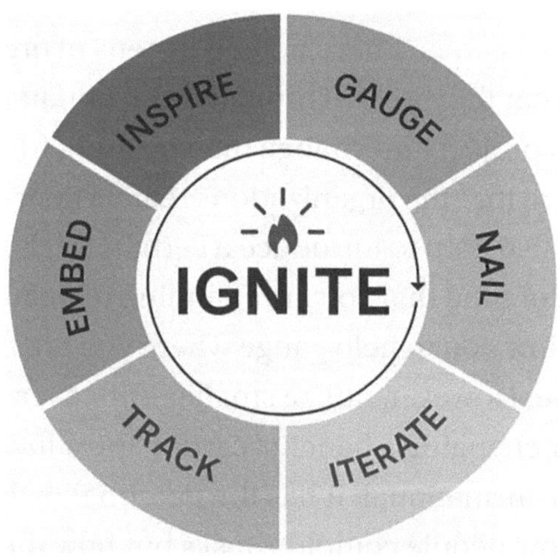

Figure 1-1. *The IGNITE Framework for AI Transformation*

I – Inspire

Every successful transformation starts with a story compelling enough to outlast the first burst of excitement. Your AI story must begin with an initial education on what AI is and, even more importantly, what it isn't. Even with the rise of tools like ChatGPT and Google's move to bake these capabilities into its flagship products like Search, AI still causes plenty of confusion. Some people fear AI as something that will take away their job; others are welcoming it with open arms in the hope that it will allow them to focus on more higher-value work.

The challenge is, everyone's starting point is quite different; therefore, as part of your project, you will need to meet people where they are. You can't underestimate the importance of providing a baseline education as to what AI is, both inside your organization and also touching on examples that they may encounter in their personal lives. Despite the very large number of users that have either used or actively adopted consumer-facing AI technologies like ChatGPT, Perplexity, Claude, Gemini, etc., there is still a population that has not, or perhaps has but is unable to connect the dots between those popular applications and the concept of AI.

Next, when you build your story, you need to make sure it does two things at once: ground itself in the organization's strategic goals and paint a picture of how work will feel when a copilot sits beside every employee. Think crisp, human language that's meant to paint the picture of how this is going to help your organization. This isn't where you will throw in IT jargon like LLMs, Graphical Processing Units ("GPU"), vector databases, or platforms. Instead, you will provide a very clear description from "*Here's the problem we face*" to "*Here's how AI helps us solve it.*"

As part of crafting that narrative, you will want to enlist the executive sponsor or sponsors who will champion the vision, fund the pilots, and shield the team when the inevitable bumps appear. They will be able to both inform what some of that messaging may look like as well as help to amplify it through the various communication channels that exist within your organization. For organizations whose culture is driven from the top down, they are essential to helping get their departments on board with supporting your pilots, implementations, etc.

G – Gauge

With the vision set, you switch from storytelling to fact-finding to help ensure that your organization is ready to take on this initiative. This includes examining your data, permissions, risk profile, and culture to see if they can support even a modest AI pilot. You are looking for elements within your organization that may cause friction, such as redundant files, fuzzy ownership, lack of lifecycle management, compliance concerns, or teams already fatigued by tech change.

The aim is not to produce a complete inventory of all your systems, processes (or lack thereof), and data sources. The intent is to surface the handful of gaps that could derail momentum and ensure that you are aligning the best groups, processes, and use cases that will support a pilot. This data is also important to provide to your sponsors if they believe a certain business function or use case would be an ideal starting point. They may not have the full visibility into the impediments that will prevent the project team from helping them realize their vision.

It's also important to note that while many AI initiatives are driven by the Information Technology ("IT") organization, they will not be successful without the full participation of the business, including executive stakeholders. Therefore, part of your work during the Gauge phase is to also understand the current working relationship between IT and business. If there isn't a strong partnership, you may want to consider illuminating this up (carefully) to your key project stakeholders and look for ways to leverage this initiative as a first step in improving those relationships. There may be other times where perhaps you need to postpone any AI initiatives until key stakeholders from the business and IT work to improve their working relationship. It all really comes down to what you discover as part of this phase.

N – Nail Pilots

The Gauge stage told you where the landmines are; now it is time to chart a path forward. In this phase, you will pick a safe, high-value spot to plant your first flag. Nail Pilots is about choosing two or three use cases that are small enough to run fast, yet big enough to prove value. With many IT organizations being asked to do more with less, it's important to align your pilots to business outcomes. Each pilot should include a clear business goal, a definition of success with applicable metrics, and a well-defined exit criterion.

You may be asking yourself, "Do we really need to go through all this work just to experiment with AI?" And unfortunately, the answer is "Yes." I have witnessed countless projects get stuck in the pilot loop and struggle to exit it. Planning upfront will help ensure that everyone is aligned with the value of the pilot that you're looking to experiment with. You will have a definition for what success looks like, which will then feed the Track Impact phase that we'll discuss later.

Once you are aligned with the business outcome you are looking to drive, you can work with your IT stakeholders to decide on the right technical solution. This conversation will also include identifying authoritative data sources, planning for the user experience, and then aligning on the right technology to bring the solution to life. Two examples of popular implementations of GenAI include both copilots and agents.

Copilots vs. Agents

When it comes to the presentation of GenAI, meaning the user interface where people will engage with technology, the two most popular patterns thus far include copilots and agents.

- **Copilots** – A chatbot-based user experience positioned as a digital assistant whereby a user can prompt to drive behaviors within the application, such as creating content or providing insights on existing content. Some examples include Microsoft 365 Copilot, Google Duet, and Adobe Firefly.
- **Agents** – GenAI applications that can be invoked by both user prompts as well as pre-configured conditions such as time, new records being created in an application, or upon receipt of a new e-mail, etc. Agents can also act "autonomously," whereby their activities are logged but not fully monitored by the user.

There's also another consideration when it comes to planning which solution best meets your use case. The typical path to introducing GenAI to an organization that I've seen usually starts with copilots and then grows to agents as people become more comfortable with the technology. Copilots tend to be less "scary" from an existential threat perspective, as the operator ultimately has full control over the actions. Agents, on the other hand, can work semi-autonomously, meaning that they don't require as much oversight from a human to interact. Between the marketing being put behind agents and the eagerness of those in Big Tech to capitalize on this new capability, agents pose a risk to workers.

I – Iterate Fast: Learning Loops

A pilot that launches on Monday can be obsolete by next Friday if it ignores feedback. Iterate Fast keeps the project alive by baking in short learning loops to collect quantitative metrics and qualitative observations as close to real time as possible. Fast, high-quality feedback is the fuel for your learning loops and is what will help you understand not only what elements of your solution can be improved but also what elements may not be a fit. This is very similar to the concept of "failing fast"; you don't want to wait too long to collect feedback to pivot your direction to meet the needs of your users.

Each loop is a chance to sharpen the model, fix a workflow hiccup, or clarify guidance before small issues harden into bad habits. The goal is momentum, not perfection. You should focus on delivering at least one improvement every cycle to help build confidence with your users. With each improvement, you will need to again survey, analyze, and incorporate user feedback into the next release, to ensure you are continuing to create business value. Remember, too, that showing users that their feedback is being heard and incorporated into upcoming releases is yet another way to help create buy-in for even some of your most challenging users.

T – Track Impact

Good stories sell change; measurable impact keeps them funded. Track Impact means building a simple KPI stack the business can trust, such as usage, quality, and headline outcomes like hours saved or revenue protected. Start with metrics you can collect without a ton of effort; then, you can graduate to dashboards that blend quantitative and qualitative data together to help further tell your story. It's important when working with your IT team to understand if there are any quantitative metrics that will be captured to help assist you with reporting out this progress. For off-the-shelf packages such as Microsoft 365 Copilot, there are both built-in analytics provided by Microsoft as well as third-party options to consider. If your solution is being developed in-house, it's important to confirm with the development team that they will be capturing metrics as part of their solution.

For some use cases or roles where the work is variable, it may be challenging to accurately measure the impact. You may have to rely on self-reporting and qualitative feedback to help paint the picture of the total impact of your solution. This is true for some technologies, such as

ChatGPT Enterprise and Microsoft 365 Copilot, where the target persona is knowledge workers who tend to have a workload that varies greatly depending on the day. Therefore, it is especially important for you to be planful when it comes to capturing qualitative feedback from your users.

In terms of capturing some of the qualitative feedback, you will want to factor in company culture and user preferences as well when it comes to how you collect that data. Some individuals will take the time to provide thoughtful feedback in writing through a survey; others may be more apt to provide that feedback through a five-to-ten-minute interview session. Understanding preferences will go a long way in ensuring that you have detailed feedback that can be actioned upon and included in future iterations of the solution, in addition to serving as input to the data that you will be sharing with your senior leadership stakeholders about the overall business impact.

Once you have collected your impact metrics that share results in plain language, executives see progress and frontline teams see their effort paying off. When the numbers paint the picture of a positive impact on your business, resistance fades to the investment made. We'll dig deeper into strategies for storytelling as it comes to reporting on impact later in this book.

E – Embed Governance and Culture

Pilots end; habits last. Embed Governance and Culture locks the gains by turning ad hoc rules into an operating model that people will need to follow. This is by far one of the most challenging stages of the IGNITE framework and requires a tremendous amount of care and feeding. Again, the objective behind any transformation is not the implementation of the backend technology, but rather the creation and adherence to the new way of working.

As much as your technical team may focus on the technical architecture for your AI initiatives, it's the business architecture that is just as important, if not more so. Business architecture, if you are unfamiliar with the term, is the high-level blueprint that connects an organization's strategy to the capabilities and value streams it must operate. It clarifies what the business needs to do, who owns each piece, and why each capability matters to delivering results. When it comes to AI transformation efforts, it is very important to ensure the initiative targets real business problems and delivers measurable results instead of becoming a technology experiment.

Now, while the business architecture sets the blueprint for the needs, the operating model is what turns that blueprint into repeatable, measurable execution within your organization. A simple example of an operating model can be seen in Figure 1-2, which outlines the people, process, and technology needed to help deliver a quote-to-order business process. As you can imagine, modifying existing business processes to incorporate change is a very change-heavy activity since it too will require people to change the way they work and build new habits to support these updates.

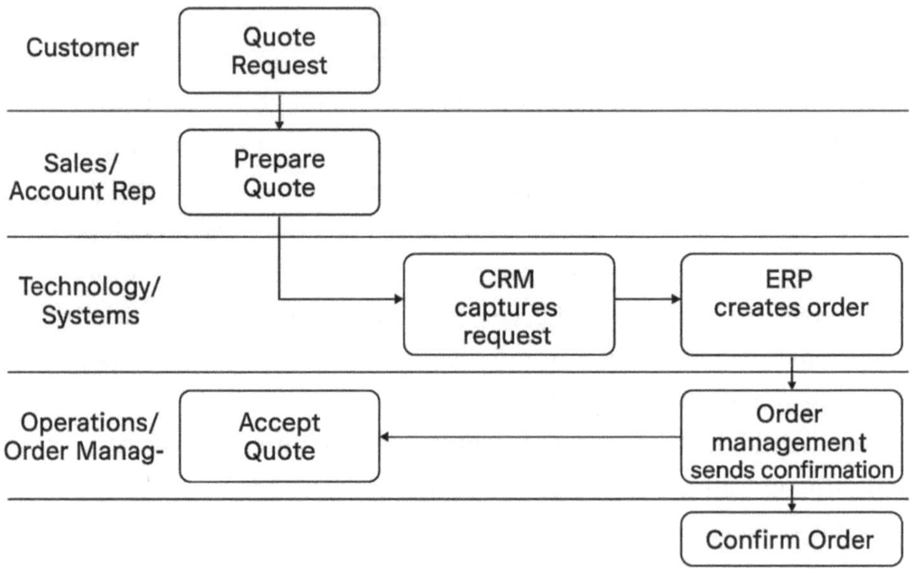

***Figure 1-2.** An Example of a Quote-to-Order Operating Model*

Define who owns prompts, data quality, and policy updates. Schedule periodic reviews so guardrails evolve with the tech. Pair governance with culture cues—champion networks, recognition for AI-assisted wins, and clear language about augmentation over replacement. When structure and mindset line up, AI stops being a project and becomes part of how the organization works every day.

Preparing for Change

While GenAI might spark excitement for technologists, it may be viewed as unsettling for others. Some people worry about job loss, biased outputs, and a loss of human judgment. For some folks, their first instinct may be to resist or work around the new tools. Recognizing that hesitation early is critical because opposition left unaddressed can stall pilots, seed misinformation, and derail investment. The starting point for any AI rollout is, therefore, empathy: acknowledge the fear, explain what the technology can and cannot do, and show how it augments rather than replaces human expertise.

Change managers turn that empathy into action. They set clear guardrails for data privacy, define new roles and skills, and create feedback loops that let users shape the road map. As you partner with IT to launch small, low-risk experiments that deliver quick wins and build momentum, then scale only when safeguards are proven. Through open communication, hands-on training, and visible executive sponsorship, you, as change managers, can help transform GenAI from a perceived threat into a trusted co-worker and reinforce your own value as the bridge between innovation and adoption. This book will cover strategies for ultimately building your change management plan for your AI transformation and then bringing it to life by leveraging the IGNITE framework.

IDENTIFYING GENAI USE CASES

One of the first exercises that many organizations take when evaluating AI is to identify impactful use cases. A great way to do this is to hold a workshop that helps to both educate on what AI is and how it works and provide example use cases for your industry. Ideally, you will have cross-representation from your business stakeholders. An example agenda for the workshop is as follows:

- **Introductions** – A quick overview of each person's name, role, tenure with the company, and a fun fact.
- **GenAI Overview** – An overview of what GenAI is, how it works, and example technologies such as ChatGPT and Microsoft Copilot.

- **Industry Examples** – Share examples of GenAI use cases that are industry relevant. Most of the hyper-scalers such as Microsoft, Google, and Oracle have these available on their websites.
- **Group Exercise** – For the remainder of the workshop, you'll run an exercise where teams surface high-value GenAI use cases by forcing unexpected combinations of business tasks, pain points, and data sources.

The Setup

Prior to the workshop, you will want to secure index cards that will be used to support this card-based exercise. You'll need to create 20–30 cards with the following categories:

- **Task** - One verb + object per card ("Create social media post," "Validate claim," "Create quote," etc.)
- **Data Source** - Internal data sources within your organization (CRM, ERP, Microsoft 365, HRIS, etc.)
- **Pain-point** - Common frustrations that exist within this process ("Very time-consuming," "Error-prone," "Annoying process," etc.)

Additionally, you will want to secure stickers that will be used for voting for the best use cases.

The Execution

Break up the participants into groups of three to five individuals. Shuffle each deck and then place the cards face down in stacks on a table. Have each team select one card from each of the three categories. Next, they'll have 20–25 minutes to identify

- Which individuals (personas or departments) are involved in this process?
- How might GenAI potentially alleviate some of the pain-points associated with this task?
- How would success be measured?

In the spirit of competition, you can also choose to either allow them to trade cards with another group or pick a new card or trade with another group if they get stuck ideating. The goal during the brainstorming will be to pull together a very quick "elevator pitch" that frames up the problem statement of who is experiencing the pain-point and the data sources that will be leveraged. Each group will have two to three minutes to present their idea and then write their group number and use case on a piece of paper.

Everyone will have three stickers that can be used for voting on the idea that they believe is the best. The top idea or ideas can then be evaluated further by the appropriate technical and business owners for GenAI. The intent of this exercise is to help break habitual thinking in a playful activity to help surface nonobvious use cases for GenAI. It also serves as a great learning experience to help introduce GenAI to individuals in your organization.

Key Takeaways

In this chapter, we saw how large language models create value through content creation and summarization; learned why the real work lies in shaping data, processes, and people; and mapped out the six-step IGNITE framework that will carry us from pilot spark to embedded practice. Keep three guardrails in view as you progress: inspire with a clear business story, measure every experiment against outcomes that matter, and cement progress with governance that protects both data and culture. Follow them, and the pilots you launch will not stall—they will build the momentum we need. In Chapter 2, we will continue our journey by focusing on one of the most important steps, building your business case for AI.

CHAPTER 2

The Business Case for AI

The Business Case for AI

With all the hype surrounding AI, it's important to remember that businesses are still accountable to shareholders, investors, and their employees to turn around a profit. Therefore, as enticing as AI might sound, it will still require a business case to fund the investment. Depending on your organization, there will be different requirements for building these business cases along with a variety of internal review processes. As someone that has helped create business cases for dozens of organizations, the only constant that I can share is that every organization handles business case reviews wildly differently.

You may find that certain investment thresholds can potentially dictate different approval levels, as well as levels of detail required to help justify the investment. Therefore, it is important to understand how business cases are managed within your organization. If this is your first business case, you will want to seek out mentorship from someone that has successfully taken an initiative through the review process so that you can hopefully replicate their success.

J. Matfess, *Your New Colleague is a Copilot*, Inside Copilot,
https://doi.org/10.1007/979-8-8688-2619-1_2

In this chapter, we are going to review the common business patterns for AI that will influence how you structure your business case. Then, we'll step through the core elements found in most business cases. Next, we'll work on identifying stakeholders that can help influence the approval of your business case and support your initiative. Then, finally, we will work on creating your AI Vision Statement that will help serve as a key form of storytelling for getting your business case approved. This AI Vision Statement is also a key component as described in the IGNITE framework we covered in Chapter 1. So, let's get started with stepping through the common business case patterns for AI.

Business Case Patterns for AI

As organizations have begun to experiment with introducing AI, there have been a couple of common patterns, as identified by Gartner, that have emerged in business cases. These patterns can be used to help guide you with how to frame your own business case, along with the language. Depending upon your review process, it might also be helpful to share these patterns with your stakeholders as part of your storytelling. These patterns include

- **Return on Employee** - This is where you are making an investment in AI as an investment for the overall happiness and benefit of the employee that is using it.
- **Return on Investment** - This pattern is where there is a quantifiable business benefit, typically aligned to a business process.
- **Return on the Future** - This is where you are making an investment in a future product or service that has yet to be developed or monetized.

Return on Employee

Transparently, return on employee is perhaps one of the most challenging business case patterns to develop. Inherently, you are making an investment in the individual employee to help improve their quality of work life. There isn't a single process or set of processes that can be measured, and depending on the target persona or employee population, it might be equally challenging to quantify the impact. However, there are several important reasons for investing in your employees that have a direct impact on your bottom line, including but not limited to

> **Employee Retention** - There is a lot of cost associated with acquiring new talent to help complete work with your organization. That cost includes not only the individuals that perform the recruiting but also the outside parties that search for niche roles and the time invested in interviewing candidates, following up, creating the offer letters, and supporting the onboarding. There is also a significant cost in helping train someone up to be effective in their role. Learning isn't just the inputs and outputs for their job function, but it also encompasses learning the organization's values, culture, language, and taxonomy. When an employee separates from an organization, it's not just the human capital that is leaving but all the knowledge and experience gained that will require effort to ramp up someone to operate at a similar level.
>
> **Talent Recruitment** - In a similar vein to employee retention and being able to keep employees happy, there is also the benefit of being able to recruit

top talent to your organization. There have been studies about the younger generations and how they look more critically at employers and tend to jump around when certain working conditions are not met. With AI being a new capability that has the potential impact of streamlining manual tasks and freeing up time to focus on high-value creative work, younger workers will congregate toward organizations that invest in this capability vs. those who do not.

Employee Development – AI is the future, but similar to when personal computers first entered the workforce, there is a learning curve to help best take advantage of this new capability. We are entering that same paradigm where businesses need to invest in AI to help skill-up their workforce to be able to take advantage of this capability in the long run. The word "experiment" is used quite frequently when talking about AI initiatives because not everything is known just yet. AI is evolving at an unprecedented rate, whereby certain limitations of today are being solved for in weeks, not months and years, as we have seen with other technologies.

There are some examples of other technologies that fall into the same category of Return on Employees, such as Employee Intranets, supporting remote access to e-mail and other collaboration services, and knowledge management solutions. These projects tend to be targeted at the knowledge workers category of employees, meaning that they typically work in back office functions such as Human Resources, Information Technology, Marketing, etc. There isn't always that quantifiable measurement of productivity gains, but there is some assumption based on industry trends and studies that these technologies help increase employee productivity without providing an exact number for what the impact is on the bottom line.

One way for you to consider quantifying the potential impact that AI may have is through a high-level impact table to help combine both the quantitative and qualitative measures for your solution. What you will do is identify the target personas for your AI application and then list out their full-time equivalent ("FTE") rates, which would be an estimate of salary plus benefits. Note that this isn't meant to be an exact number as actual salaries are going to vary based on years of experience, work locations, and other factors. However, typically, from my experience, most senior stakeholders understand that point.

Next, you can start to forecast the potential time that this may help them save per week. You should estimate conservatively, as AI is still very much an emerging capability. Overpromising potential cost savings could put you in a situation where you need to defend your position more than if you start with a more modest starting point. To help back that up, you can also remind your executive stakeholders that AI is still an emerging capability, and there may even be some initial productivity decreases in the beginning as employees begin to onboard. The FTE rate combined with the estimated number of hours per week your solution will help save is what makes up the quantifiable financial impact of your solution.

From there, you will want to provide placeholders for what the qualitative impacts might be. In other words, what are the other downstream impacts that you anticipate realizing through the investment in this technology. Some common examples of this would include a noticeable improvement in the quality of products and services delivered. Other organizations with strong people culture may look to measure how this may impact their employee satisfaction scores and retention rates. Others might also be interested in anecdotal examples of how this impacts work/life balance, or other aspects of their overall work experience.

BRAINSTORMING EMPLOYEE-CENTRIC AI BENEFITS

When it comes to identifying qualitative measures, it is best to enlist help from a cross-representation of employees from the department or departments you intend on targeting, along with representatives from an employee-focused department such as Human Resources ("HR"). This is one of those examples where bringing HR into the effort early could really prove to help you in the long run. This doesn't have to be a huge exercise, maybe just 30 minutes where folks get together either in a conference room or through a virtual meeting.

First, you will want to review any important business goals or metrics that your senior leadership has set forth. Some example goals that your organization may already have could include the following:

- Grow revenue faster than headcount.
- Reduce cost to serve per customer or ticket.
- Lower data leakage and overexposure risk.
- Improve employee engagement and reduce burnout.
- Increase decision speed and quality.

For each of those organizational goals, you can then start to brainstorm what the potential benefits of introducing AI are to help drive you toward those goals. This may require you to further unpack the high-level goals into more smaller goals—for example, you may look at the "reduce cost to serve per customer or ticket" and start to identify ways of impacting that metric while also supporting your employees. During your brainstorming, you might focus on areas of friction. Some stakeholders might immediately look at that metric and assume that the value of AI would be to reduce the number of humans that support your customer base; however, that isn't really an employee-centric view of how AI can help.

Rather, you should focus on the aspects of the contact center representative role that incur friction and position AI to support that. For example, if AI could help better provide recommendations during the call for resolution steps based on the customer's history with your company, that may have the double benefit of improving the customer experience while also helping to assist the contact center employee. Improving that one particular goal could have a downstream impact as well, of addressing your "grow revenue faster than headcount" by reducing customer churn while also perhaps increasing the number of upsell opportunities.

There's no set time limit for how long you should conduct this brainstorming exercise, but usually, 30–45 minutes should suffice. Again, the intent is less about coming up with all the answers during this exercise, but rather for you to identify opportunities to perform further research.

Once you have assembled these estimates, you can put together a slide with a table similar to Table 2-1 to help articulate to your senior stakeholders what you are striving for in terms of an impact or return on your investment. You will want to note that these are considered to be a starting point and that some of the estimates will need to be self-reported through surveys, interviews, etc. This should hopefully help support those inevitable conversations that will come up regarding what your organization should expect to realize through investing in your project from a return on employee perspective.

Table 2-1. AI Business Impact Analysis Table

Persona	FTE Rate	Time Savings per week	Cost Impact (monthly)	Quality Improvement	Job Satisfaction
Project Manager	$55	3	$660	65%	45%
Business Analyst	$45	3	$540	80%	75%
Contact Center Manager	$35	2	$280	55%	30%
Recruiter	$60	1	$156	35%	20%
Finance Manager	$65	1	$240	40%	60%

Return on Investment

The next category of business case is where there is a quantifiable return on investment ("ROI"). A great example of where you can build a business case with an ROI is in a contact center. Contact centers are perhaps one of the most measured functions within any organization that has a customer service component to it. There is a litany of metrics captured, including call volume, average call time, staffing levels, peak call hours, and call volume per contact center employee. We interact with contact centers in many facets of our lives, in everything from addressing a discrepancy on your electricity bill, rebooking travel if your flight is cancelled, or filing a claim with your insurance company.

Organizations recognize the importance of this function from the ability to both quickly service their customers and ensure that the experience is positive to help retain their business. Therefore, many organizations look to improve this process through technology by offering automated call menus with self-service functions, enabling you to request a callback vs. waiting on hold, etc. These investments help improve the customer experience and, in some cases, can enable a company to reduce the number of contact center agents that they have working. The fewer individuals performing the work, the less cost incurred by the organization, which ultimately impacts the bottom line.

If you were working on what an ROI might be for an AI solution meant to support the contact center function, you would most likely start with

- **Average Call Time** - What's the impact on the average time a contact center agent spends helping a customer?
- **Customer Satisfaction** - Assuming your contact center includes an after-call survey, are customers more satisfied with the service they have received after implementing your solution?
- **Contact Center Staffing Levels** - Assuming that the average call time drops and the customer satisfaction scores stay where they are or improve, a case could be made that you might be able to cut back on employees performing this work, which could potentially result in a positive ROI, assuming the technology costs are less than the human capital.

Return on the Future

In some instances, investing in AI might not result in an immediate return but is necessary for the longevity of your business. A notable example of this is the pharmaceutical industry. The process for introducing a new drug to market is a multi-year, if not decade-long, endeavor. AI could potentially help in multiple aspects of this process, including scientific research, testing, etc., which would all potentially support a quantifiable ROI. But AI also may be able to help discover new medical advances that might not have previously been possible. It can do so by analyzing massive datasets at super-human speed, uncovering patterns that inspire new hypotheses for experimental validation.

Also, staying with that same use case of accelerating research and development, there is the potential to automate routine lab work and continuously synthesize the latest literature. This shift of taking on the more mundane aspects of research can help free scientists up to focus on creative questions and cross-disciplinary collaboration. This return on the future may follow a similar pattern to what your company may follow for funding research and development initiatives. Developing hypotheses and then proving them out is a key step in driving innovation and helping to bring new products and services to market. If your company has a research and development department, it may be worth exploring how they tend to quantify return on the future and to see if there are any templates or examples that you can leverage.

No matter if you are focused on return on employee, return on investment, or return on the future, eventually you will need to put that vision together to share with executive leadership. That leads us to our next big topic to cover, building your business case for AI.

Typical Elements of a Business Case

It's important to once again stress that all businesses are vastly different in how they approach developing business cases. Therefore, the guidance provided here may not be fully inclusive of your organization's requirements; consequently, it is best to consult with your management team to ensure that your list is complete.

However, to get started, I might suggest you consider leveraging GenAI to assist you with starting to build your business case. One of the benefits of doing so is you can both work and learn along the way.

For example, you could ask ChatGPT, "What's typically in a business case?" and then review the response back, which for me is as follows:

1. **Executive Summary**

   Short overview: problem or opportunity, recommended option, cost, expected return, and decision needed.

2. **Problem/Opportunity Statement**

   What business pain or missed opportunity are we solving? Note who is affected, the current impact, and urgency.

3. **Strategic Alignment**

   Show how the proposal supports company strategy, goals, regulatory needs, customer commitments, or transformation priorities.

4. **Objectives and Scope**

   Define what success looks like. Clarify in-scope and out-of-scope items to prevent expectation creep.

5. **Options Analysis**

   Lay out viable alternatives (status quo, build, buy, partner, phased, etc.). Compare on cost, value, time, risk, and complexity.

6. **Recommended Option**

   State the choice and why it wins. Tie back to value, speed, compliance fit, total cost, and risk profile.

7. **Benefits**

    - **Financial (Quantified)** - Revenue growth, cost avoidance, cost reduction, efficiency gains, capacity expansion.
    - **Nonfinancial (Qualitative)** - Customer satisfaction, risk reduction, employee experience, data quality, compliance posture.

      Translate as many as possible into measurable impact.

8. **Cost Model and Funding Plan**

    Capex vs. opex. One-time vs. recurring. Licensing, staffing, change management, training, support, integration, and data cleanup. Note the funding source and budget timing.

9. **Financial Analysis**

    Use the methods your organization expects: NPV, IRR, payback period, TCO comparison, and breakeven volumes. Show assumptions and sensitivity ranges.

10. **Risks, Issues, and Mitigations**

    Implementation, adoption, vendor, security, compliance, dependency, and data quality. Rate impact and likelihood. Assign mitigation owners.

11. **Assumptions and Constraints**

    List key dependencies (resources, timelines, data access, executive sponsorship). Call out constraints such as regulation, tooling limits, and contracts.

12. **Implementation Approach and Timeline**

    Phases, major milestones, critical path tasks, resource model (internal vs partner), and gating criteria between phases.

13. **Change Management and Adoption Plan**

    Communications, training, champions, user readiness, support, and post go-live reinforcement. Tie to adoption metrics.

14. **Stakeholder Impact and RACI**

    Identify who is affected, decisions they own, and their roles in delivery and operations. Include a RACI or similar matrix.

15. **Success Metrics and KPIs**

    Define how success will be measured: usage, cost savings realized, cycle time reductions, compliance scores, NPS, etc. Include baseline and target.

16. **Governance and Reporting**

    Explain how progress, spend, and outcomes will be tracked. Include cadence for steering reviews and escalation path.

17. **Decision Request**

    Be explicit: approve funding, staff allocation, vendor contract, pilot, or phase gate. Include amount, timeframe, and any conditions.

18. **Appendixes (As Needed)**

    Detailed financial models, technical architecture, vendor quotes, regulatory mapping, data inventory, risk register, market research, and pilot results.

Quick Build Tips

- Keep the main body skimmable for executives; move details to appendixes.
- Include a one-page option scorecard.
- Tie benefits to metrics leadership already tracks.
- Show the cost of doing nothing.
- Make assumptions explicit so reviewers can test the model.

It might feel awkward to leverage AI to help create a business case for AI, but that's precisely how you should be using this technology. As we discussed earlier, GenAI has been trained on all sorts of documents. Therefore, as shown in this example, it is aware of what a business case is and the typical deliverables included within. As someone that has spent many years building business cases both in industry and as a consultant, I can suggest that all the areas that ChatGPT provided are quite applicable to many business cases that I have put together. Your organization's requirements for a business case may differ slightly.

Also, remember that not only can AI help you with understanding what exists within a business case, but it can also help you with drafting content for each of these deliverables.

Crafting a Vision Statement

One of the deliverables that ChatGPT didn't specify, but is incredibly helpful at helping sell your idea within your organization, is a Vision Statement. The Vision Statement's main purpose is to paint the picture of what life will look like after you have implemented this new solution. Often, the Vision Statement is included in the Executive Summary, as what you are ultimately doing is a form of storytelling to help get buy-in and drive excitement for your project. As someone that has come from consulting, I often explain that your vision statement is what you use to sell your ideas to others as a means to gain buy-in and approval to move forward.

The challenge, of course, is in the beginning, you might not know exactly what the true capabilities of AI are; you might need to develop a hypothesis for what it can do and help explain that as part of your business plan. The goal, though, is to think big and help create a narrative that is compelling. You also should consider that your project alone might not completely solve the business problem completely from end-to-end.

For example, imagine you are a nonprofit organization that is focused on raising awareness of hunger and helps raise money to supplement food banks. Your vision for an investment in AI might be broken down into

- How this solution might help improve the lives of the people working or volunteering their time at your nonprofit
- The processes you intend to impact, such as community outreach, or serving the needs of those who you support
- The new outcomes you intend to drive through this investment, such as increasing donations or the community that your nonprofit serves

EXERCISE: CREATING YOUR VISION STATEMENT

A popular exercise I have used to help organizations develop a vision statement is centered on focusing on the future after successfully completing a project. This is often called building your "future press release" or "front-page headline from the future." You write the celebratory news story as if the initiative already succeeded, then work backward to make it real. This exercise will also help with fleshing out other aspects of your business case.

Headline (pick one): [Company] achieves [quantified outcome] by [timeframe]

Subhead: In [period], [audience] realized [benefit] after [key change]
Lede (3–4 sentences):

- What changed
- For whom
- Why it matters to the business
- When it happened

Results at a Glance:

- [Metric 1]: went from A to B
- [Metric 2]: went from A to B
- [Risk/compliance]: from A to B
- [Adoption or satisfaction]: X%, net promoter score up by Y points

Quotes: Customer: "*This helped save me 2 hours/week!*"Employee: "*I really appreciate how quickly they got back to me, and with the exact information that I needed.*"

What We Deliberately Did Not Do:

- *What business areas, processes, or user bases were perhaps left out of scope for this project*

What's Next:

- *Examples of what other areas of your business might impact from this solution, or perhaps what might be the next AI solution you will look to deliver after this project.*

From this exercise, you can distill your future press release into a very simple vision statement using the following format:

Vision Statement (one liner): We [enable who] to [do what] so they can [outcome] with [distinctive edge].

For example: *We enable every donor to see their impact clearly so they can give more confidently with AI-personalized engagement.*

Key Takeaways

In this chapter, we covered how to build an AI business case leaders can act on: start by stating the problem in the language of existing organizational goals; choose the return you will anchor on (return on employee, return on investment, or return on the future); lay out real options, including doing nothing, and show the cost of delay; quantify what you can and qualify what you cannot; make risks, controls, ownership, and measurement plans explicit; note assumptions, dependencies, and change management needs; use GenAI to draft, structure, and pressure test the case, not to replace your judgment; and close with a simple vision statement or future press release that helps people see the win. The goal is to give executives a clear decision and a clear path to measure and scale.

CHAPTER 3

Gauge Your Readiness

Before you can ignite change, you need to gauge what could go wrong.

Evaluating Data, Operational, and Cultural Risks

Artificial intelligence has reignited a wave of transformation unlike anything we have seen since the introduction of the internet or the public cloud. Yet the organizations seeing the most success are not necessarily the ones with the biggest budgets or most sophisticated models. They are the ones that first gauged their readiness and built an actionable plan to address their gaps. They understood that every innovation carries risk: the risk of misuse, of misinterpretation, of overreliance, or of under-preparedness.

The Gauge phase of the IGNITE framework is about taking a structured look at where those risks live in your organization. It is about assessing not just whether the technology will work, but whether your organization is ready for it to work responsibly. Like other large-scale transformation efforts, AI adoption demands a coordinated mix of technical preparedness,

J. Matfess, *Your New Colleague is a Copilot*, Inside Copilot,
https://doi.org/10.1007/979-8-8688-2619-1_3

operational discipline, and cultural acceptance. Many leaders discover that their biggest roadblocks are not the models or the APIs. They are the people, the data, and the policies.

When I work with organizations beginning their AI journey, three consistent themes always emerge as the flashpoints for readiness: **data**, **operations**, and **culture.** Each represents a different dimension of risk that must be managed before you can move from experimentation to enterprise scale.

This chapter reframes AI readiness through the lens of organizational risk. We will explore how:

- **Data Risk** - Determines what AI can and should see
- **Operational Risk** - Shapes how AI behaves under governance
- **Cultural Risk** - Whether people will trust and adopt it

Together, these form your **AI Risk Readiness Map**, a framework you can use to evaluate where your organization stands and what actions you will need to take before lighting the fuse of innovation. Additionally, this map will help you to identify areas within your organization that may be more accepting of this risk to help inform where you may start from a "Pilot project" perspective. However, for now, let's go ahead and start exploring these different areas of risk.

Data Risk: Knowing What AI Can and Should See

There is a saying that is as old as computing itself: "Garbage in, garbage out." Nowhere is that truer than in artificial intelligence. Data is both AI's jet fuel and its kryptonite, the source of its power and the root of its most dangerous mistakes. When people first experience generative AI, they are amazed by how much it seems to "know." But AI does not truly know anything; it predicts the desired outcome you are looking for. It draws from the data it has been trained or grounded on. That means your organization's AI outcomes are only as reliable as the data you feed them.

To gauge readiness, you must first start by understanding your data risk landscape: where your business information lives, how it is governed, and how much of it should be visible to AI at all. This will not only help you prepare for the first initial AI pilots or proof-of-concept efforts but also serve as a pulse-check for determining how much effort might be required to become a true AI-enabled organization.

The Anatomy of Data Risk

Every organization manages at a minimum two main types of data: structured and unstructured. We will unpack both data types for what they are and some of the key considerations for you to be aware of when targeting these data sources for your AI use cases.

Structured data is the neat, orderly kind that lives in enterprise systems such as ERP, CRM, and HRIS platforms. It is formatted, validated, and usually subject to formal governance. When managed well, it provides trustworthy metrics that help leaders make key decisions about the overall business. Typically, structured data sources are considered "sources of truth" in organizations, and senior leaders often make decisions based on the data housed in these systems. But even here, risk hides in the details. Duplicate records, inconsistent naming conventions, and gaps in data curation can distort reports and mislead downstream AI models.

Imagine a global software company selling to Microsoft through multiple regional teams. In its Customer Resources Management ("CRM") platform, the account might appear under half a dozen variations: Microsoft, Microsoft Corp., Microsoft APAC, The Microsoft Corporation. For a human, the connection is obvious. For AI, it is not. When an AI assistant queries "Show all Microsoft opportunities," the system could miscount or double-count, depending on which entity it pulls from. Inconsistent data erodes trust, and trust is the foundation AI depends on.

That's just the AI experience, but the problem also manifests for humans. If sales representatives start to create opportunities across those multiple account objects, it can be challenging as a business to understand what your sales pipeline looks like per company without standardization, since the reports would show leads across multiple companies that are really Microsoft. This can also lead to other challenges, such as sales representatives not realizing that they're talking with the same customer or perhaps even selling to the same customer. This is just a small example but hopefully helps paint the picture of how data governance with structured data sources can have an impact.

Unstructured data, by contrast, is the digital junk drawer of modern organizations. It is sprawling, messy, and everywhere: buried in email attachments, file shares, Teams chats, Google Drives, SharePoint sites, and old network folders that no one remembers owning. There is valuable insight in there, but it is tangled up with outdated documents, duplicate files, and sensitive information that probably should not be shared.

Unstructured data risk typically shows up in three ways:

1. **Volume risk** - There is simply too much of it to manage effectively at scale.
2. **Visibility risk** - No one knows what is in it or who can see it, and it is rapidly changing on a week-to-week basis.
3. **Validity risk** - Much of it is obsolete or untrustworthy.

Left unchecked, these risks can sabotage any progress you may hope to make with your AI initiatives. If your copilot or agent is grounding answers on unreviewed, overshared content, it may reveal confidential material, propagate outdated policies, or generate hallucinations that look authoritative but are simply wrong.

Data Risk in the Age of RAG and Fine-Tuning

When you begin integrating your business data with AI, you will likely face a key decision: whether to use Retrieval-Augmented Generation ("RAG") or fine-tuning as your technical approach. Each method carries different kinds of data risk and unique dependencies in terms of remediation efforts to attempt to mitigate these risks. Let's explore these two technical approaches further and then discuss some of the change management and business efforts that will be needed to bring these to life.

RAG dynamically retrieves relevant documents and passes them to a large language model for context. For example, you may have a Google Workspace with IT Policies and Procedures. If you were to prompt Google Gemini with what's the policy for ordering a new laptop, it will take your prompt and first try to deduce the intent of what you're looking for. Next, it'll access the search index and try to pull in data that will further ground the response based on the access that you have. This approach is relatively fast to implement and respects existing permissions but depends entirely on the quality and governance of your document repositories.

Fine-tuning retrains a model on curated, domain-specific data. It can produce more consistent, specialized results but requires intense effort to collect, clean, and approve every data point used for training, along with ongoing retraining when your information changes. These options of retrieval augmented generation (RAG) and fine-tuning are outlined in Table 3-1.

***Table 3-1.** Retrieval Augment Generation vs. Fine-Tuning*

Approach	How It Works	Setup Effort	Typical Use Case
Retrieval-Augmented Generation (RAG)	The user's prompt is first analyzed for intent. Next, the application performs a semantic search and then retrieves the most relevant documents, which are fed back to the model as context.	Low – Your content is indexed using a search indexer, your content, and set up connectors.	Knowledge bases, productivity copilots/agents.
Fine-Tuning	A pre-trained model such as GPT-5 is further trained on a curated, domain-specific dataset.	High – You will need to collect, clean, label, and format data sets; run experiment cycles.	Industry-specific chatbots, regulated scenarios

The right choice depends on your use case, but either way, the data readiness work is unavoidable. This is perhaps one of the most overlooked steps in preparing for an AI project, as data governance and data security remediation are not considered to be "exciting" new work but rather are needed to address the lack of historical funding and attention.

Note Fine-tuning may not be feasible when you lack a large, high-quality dataset, since small or inconsistent data can cause the model to overfit and perform worse. It can also be impractical due to the significant computational cost, operational complexity, and slow retraining cycles required to maintain a fine-tuned model over time.

Content Readiness As a Change Initiative

The most important point for you to walk away with is RAG thrives on well-governed repositories. Unfortunately, few organizations can honestly describe their data that way. Unstructured content is often decades old, stored with lax permissions, and owned by no one. So many organizations found themselves rushing to migrate their on-premises file shares and SharePoint instances to cloud-based document collaboration platforms. Typically, this was performed as a "lift and shift," meaning that little effort was made to curate the content for its new cloud repository. This means your first AI pilot will quickly expose the cracks in your information architecture, or lack thereof.

For you to begin remediating for this lack of governance, you will need to treat this as a change initiative, and not just a technical one. You will need to work with data owners to clean, classify, and secure the content that AI will access. This is likely going to be viewed as unplanned work for these data owners, so part of the effort will be to educate them on not just the "why" behind this effort but also how they will be impacted both positively and negatively. To explain the effort in plain terms, it might be helpful to posit that if you would not publish it on your website or intranet site, your AI probably should not be reading it either.

This will hopefully help them address not only the lax permissions that exist within their sites and collaboration spaces but also the quality of the data out there. Tapping into the junk drawer analogy, it is important for them to consider this yearly cleanup exercise where they review not only access but also the redundant, outdated, and trivial ("ROT") data that exists within their sites. For example, if Human Resources is one of your target customers, you should help reiterate that the user experience that you intend on building will be able to answer questions about policies and procedures from this year and not ground responses on a document that is 5–10 years old. This preparatory work is the groundwork for trustable AI.

Clarifying Roles and Ownership

Improving data quality inevitably introduces new responsibilities. Someone has to decide which files stay, which go, and which define the source of truth. That person might not exist yet in your organization as an enterprise librarian, and this responsibility may not have been articulated to data owners when they initially requested or created a SharePoint Site or Microsoft Team to collaborate.

Clear ownership structures, even temporary ones, are critical. Data stewards, records managers, or business unit representatives can all play a role in certifying content for AI readiness. Your job as a leader is to explain why this work matters. AI magnifies whatever you give it. Neglected data does not stay hidden; it becomes amplified. Framing the cleanup effort as risk mitigation rather than administrative overhead helps shift perception. Instead of "another IT request," it becomes part of protecting the company's reputation and ensuring accurate outcomes.

Setting User Expectations

Another subtle form of data risk comes from user misunderstanding. RAG systems do not behave like ChatGPT; their answers vary because the data behind them changes. When a user asks, "Show me all policies related to travel reimbursement," the system might surface ten documents today and eight tomorrow if one file was moved or permissions changed. That is not a bug; it is a feature of live data grounding.

In addition, without proper expectation-setting, users may lose confidence in AI. Your job is to help them understand that variability is normal, that AI reflects what is currently available, and that accuracy improves as repositories become more curated. There's also the nuance of language, as these AI solutions are not performing a keyword search, but rather a semantic one, meaning that they are deciding on the potential intent of the individual performing the search. Slight variations to the words you choose in your prompt will yield different results in addition to a varying backend dataset.

Fine-tuned models, on the other hand, deliver more consistent answers but lag reality since LLM retraining is expensive and infrequent. Meaning, the effort it takes to publish a new version of your employer's benefits to an intranet site is much lower than executing a training exercise to further fine-tune an existing LLM. Either way, whether you go down the RAG route or decide to fine-tune an existing LLM, you should absolutely be transparent with communications to build trust and patience as your AI program matures.

Upskilling the Support Network

Supporting AI requires new skills across your technical teams. Help-desk analysts will need to differentiate between retrieval issues such as permissions errors or indexing gaps and model behavior such as hallucinations or outdated grounding. This is a far departure from the normal IT troubleshooting steps of asking someone to turn the underperforming device or application on, then off. Additionally, governance teams must learn to interpret AI telemetry logs and trace a model's "chain of thought." This is especially important for regulated industries or for industries that are frequently audited, as the reason behind a decision made by the organization can be scrutinized by state, local, or even federal entities.

Just as importantly, those support teams need reassurance. AI is not replacing them; it is changing the nature of their work. By equipping them with diagnostic skills and giving them early visibility into AI pilots, you turn potential skeptics into allies who can explain and defend the technology to others. One of the most popular sayings during this "AI boom" is that AI is not coming for your job, but rather people that embrace the technology are the ones that are going to put you out of work.

Governance and Compliance Alignment

No discussion of data risk is complete without addressing governance and compliance. RAG solutions operate in near-real time, based on when the data was last indexed through an enterprise search service. This means that your data-loss-prevention (DLP), role-based access control, and data classification policies must be revisited. Often, organizations have wanted to tackle these efforts but have not had the leadership support to dedicate the time or resources to make it happen. It also means revisiting your data lifecycle management processes to ensure your AI solutions are grounding on relevant information and not stale data.

Most collaboration ecosystems, especially Microsoft 365 and Google Workspace, were designed for openness and teamwork. That is their strength, but it also introduces a quiet risk: oversharing or what is sometimes referred to as over-permissioning. Oversharing occurs when documents are shared with more people than necessary or with entire groups by default. AI does not distinguish between "intended" and "allowed" access. If a user can technically see a file, AI can ground on it.

This is where proactive risk management pays off. Before scaling your pilots, partner with compliance teams to audit permissions, label sensitive data with protection policies, and validate connectors into third-party systems. The goal is not to block innovation; it is to ensure that AI operates within the same trust boundaries you already expect of your human employees.

From Data to Decision

Data readiness is not just a checkbox in your AI road map. It is the foundation for every decision, every insight, and every answer your agents will produce. Organizations that treat data as a living asset will realize far more than AI being just a novelty. It becomes a reliable partner that is able to help augment the humans that make up their business.

Organizations that skip this step often find themselves firefighting issues later, such as unexpected data exposure, inconsistent results, or user mistrust. Gauging your data risk early helps you identify weak spots before they cause harm.

Operational Risk: Managing Systems, Models, and Guardrails

While data risk determines what AI can and should see, operational risk defines how it behaves once it starts learning, retrieving, and responding. Operational risk lives at the intersection of systems, policies, and human oversight. It asks the question: "Even if our data is ready, can our infrastructure, processes, and people keep AI operating within safe and predictable limits?"

In traditional IT projects, operational risk might mean a system outage or a missed service-level agreement. In AI projects, operational risk is about consistency, explainability, and control. When models evolve, when connectors expand, or when permissions drift, the stability of your AI's responses can change in subtle but serious ways.

Understanding Operational Risk

Operational risk in AI often emerges in three forms:

1. **Systemic risk**, which comes from infrastructure, data pipelines, or connections not being monitored
2. **Model risk**, which appears when a fine-tuned model begins to drift or when grounding data becomes stale
3. **Governance risk**, which results from unclear ownership or missing review processes between IT, business, and compliance teams

These risks are interrelated. A broken connector may prevent grounding data from refreshing. That data may lead to outdated answers, which then undermine user trust. Imagine if you may that a user asks a benefits question and receives a response that is grounded on a document that is over ten years old! This will not only cause the user to distrust AI, but they may also voice their findings to others, causing a wave of distrust throughout the organization. Governance teams might not even realize that drift occurred until someone raises a complaint, making it even more difficult to address.

The best way to manage operational risk is to think about AI as a living system rather than a static application. Like any system that learns or retrieves from changing sources, it requires regular maintenance, human oversight, and clear rules for when to pause, retrain, or retire. Moderna, a biotechnology company headquartered in Cambridge, Massachusetts, best known for developing one of the first COVID-19 vaccines, recently made the notable decision to merge its HR and IT functions. They decided to create a single leadership role: the "Chief People & Digital Technology Officer," based on how they view AI, workflows, and the future of human-machine collaboration.

The Human-in-the-Loop Imperative

Despite what some of the world's largest software companies may tell you, AI will never replace the need for human judgment. It can summarize, recommend, or assist, but it should never operate without a feedback loop. In regulated industries such as healthcare or finance, every AI-assisted decision must be traceable back to its sources and reviewed by a qualified person

This concept of human-in-the-loop is not a limitation; it is your safety net. It ensures that when the model's reasoning path is unclear, someone can step in to interpret and verify the result. It also provides a learning opportunity, allowing human reviewers to feed corrections or clarifications back into your governance process. As you gauge operational readiness, make sure you have clearly defined who reviews, approves, and audits AI-generated outcomes. These checkpoints are what turn experimentation into responsible production.

Case Vignette: When a Well-Meaning AI Pilot Hit Turbulence

One of the most widely discussed real-world lessons in AI governance came from an unlikely source: an airline's website chatbot. In early 2024, Air Canada was found legally responsible for the misinformation that its automated assistant provided to a grieving customer. The chatbot had offered an inaccurate description of the company's bereavement fare policy, suggesting that the traveler could apply for a partial refund after purchasing a ticket at the regular price. When the customer later requested the refund, Air Canada refused, arguing that the chatbot had made a mistake and that its advice was not official policy.

The case, Moffatt v. Air Canada (2024 BCCRT 149), reached the British Columbia Civil Resolution Tribunal, which ruled decisively against the airline. Tribunal Member Christopher C. Rivers wrote, "It should be obvious to Air Canada that it is responsible for all the information on its website. It makes no difference whether the information comes from a static page or a chatbot." The outcome sent a clear message to every organization experimenting with AI: automation does not reduce accountability. If your AI system communicates with customers, employees, or partners, the organization owns those responses as surely as if a human had written them.

Air Canada was ordered to compensate the traveler, but the reputational damage extended much further. The story spread quickly across global media, fueling debates about transparency, human oversight, and the legal boundaries of conversational AI. For leaders preparing their own AI pilots, the Air Canada case is a cautionary reminder that AI governance is not optional once automation reaches the public.

This case also highlights the importance of verifying what your systems say, maintaining clear escalation paths when errors occur, and keeping humans involved whenever outputs have financial, legal, or emotional impact. It also reinforces a central principle of responsible AI deployment: trust is built through accountability. The moment your users believe that an AI can speak on behalf of your brand, it becomes part of your organization's voice. Therefore, this needs to be included as part of your risk profile to ensure that your customers and employees

Building Your AI Governance Playbook

Operational risk management starts with clarity. Everyone involved should understand who owns each part of the AI ecosystem and how decisions are made. A simple way to achieve this is through a **shared responsibility model** as outlined in Table 3-2.

Table 3-2. *Shared Responsibility Model for AI Governance*

Layer	Responsibilities
Platform Provider (Microsoft, OpenAI, Google, etc.)	Model security, uptime, and compliance certifications
Your Organization's IT and Security Teams	Data connectors, permissions, network security, monitoring, and cloud infrastructure
Business Data Owners	Data quality, collaboration workspace permissions, and prompts.
Compliance and Risk Teams	Risk framework for AI, retention policies, and regulatory compliance.

This model reinforces that operational risk is not owned by a single department. It is shared. IT manages the pipes, compliance defines the guardrails, and the business ensures that outputs make sense.

Mature organizations document these roles in an **AI** governance playbook. The playbook defines approved data sources, decision gates, escalation paths, and incident response workflows. It should also outline how your organization will adapt to changes in model behavior or platform updates. Think of it as a living manual that captures lessons learned from each pilot and makes them reusable for the next one.

Monitoring, Measurement, and Incident Response

Just like the humans in your organization, AI will make mistakes. What separates responsible organizations from reckless ones is how quickly they detect and respond. Establish an **AI incident response plan** just as you would for cybersecurity.

Your plan should include

1. **Detection triggers** such as user reports, abnormal query results, or compliance alerts
2. **Containment steps** like disabling a connector, revoking access, or removing a dataset
3. **Root cause analysis** to determine whether the issue came from permissions, training data, or the model itself
4. **Remediation and retraining actions** that prevent recurrence

5. **Communication protocols** for transparency with leadership and affected stakeholders

    - The goal is not to eliminate every risk, but to respond intelligently and consistently when risk appears.

Operational Readiness Checklist

As you assess operational risk, look for evidence that your organization can manage the following areas:

- Documented governance playbook and escalation procedures
- Access and connector audits completed before each pilot
- Human-in-the-loop review processes defined for regulated workflows
- Monitoring systems that log retrievals and AI outputs for audit
- Clear ownership for retraining, reindexing, and change management

If any of these items are missing, your AI environment may be running ahead of your ability to control it. The good news is that operational readiness improves quickly once these practices become routine.

Cultural Risk – Building Trust, Curiosity, and Confidence

Technology projects often fail not because the technology is flawed, but because people are not ready to change how they work. AI is no exception. Cultural risk is about how people perceive, trust, and interact with intelligent systems. It is important to note that every organization has its own culture. Some celebrate experimentation and innovation. Others are built on precision, compliance, and risk avoidance. Neither approach is wrong, but each influences how AI adoption unfolds.

For example, a manufacturing company with a strong safety culture may approach AI with cautious skepticism. Employees might ask whether automation will compromise quality or replace skilled labor. A creative agency, by contrast, may rush to use AI everywhere, only to realize later that it has no process for validating results. Both are cultural risks—one of resistance, the other of overconfidence.

Understanding the Human Side of Risk

AI has the potential to evoke powerful emotions when discussed in a work setting. For some people, it represents excitement and opportunity. For others, it triggers fear of replacement or loss of control. Leaders must address these reactions head-on. Avoiding the conversation only amplifies anxiety and can be just the thing that prevents users from wanting to participate in your AI project.

The first step in your journey to assessing the human side of risk is to start by identifying your AI champions. These are the curious individuals who are willing to experiment, share lessons, and help others learn. You may be able to repurpose a change champion group from other transformation projects, such as a new intranet or when you perhaps launched a new enterprise system. You'll want to pair these enthusiasts with trusted skeptics who can raise tough questions about ethics, accuracy, and fairness. When both groups are included, you get balanced feedback and stronger adoption.

Transparency is also an incredibly important factor to include in your AI project. Explain what data the AI uses, how it generates responses, and what safeguards are in place. The more visible your process, the more confidence people will have in the outcomes.

Creating a Learning Culture

Cultural readiness grows through learning, and this is incredibly important when talking about AI. Offer short, scenario-based training that demystifies AI instead of abstract theory. Show employees how Copilot or Gemini can draft a meeting summary, how to verify sources, and when to escalate unclear results. Focus on the benefits while also showcasing some of the limitations to help quell the fear that this new capability will be replacing them in the short-term.

You should also encourage experimentation with AI but link it to the governance practices you have in place. Give teams safe spaces, such as sandbox environments, where they can test AI features without risk to production data. When mistakes occur, you need to treat them as opportunities to learn, not reasons for punishment or a threat to discontinue the experimentation. Over time, this approach replaces fear with curiosity and compliance with confidence, as your users mature their understanding of the technology.

Measuring Cultural Readiness

There are a couple of steps that you can take to help gauge cultural risk through a few targeted questions:

- How often do employees voluntarily use AI tools in their daily work?
- Do team meetings include discussions about AI ethics, results, or improvements?
- Is there a clear channel for reporting errors or concerns?
- Are leaders modeling responsible AI usage themselves?

When AI becomes part of the daily conversation rather than a side project, your organization has moved from curiosity to capability. This is the critical path to maturing from "we are experimenting with AI and trying out our first initial use case" to "we are transforming our organization to include AI in our flow of work."

Workshop: Building Your AI Readiness Heat Map

Every organization will have strengths and weaknesses across the three dimensions of risk. The goal of this exercise is to visualize those differences and prioritize action, using Table 3-3 as your reference.

Table 3-3. *AI Readiness Heat Map*

Risk Domain	Key Question	Rating (1–5)	Notes
Data	Do we know which repositories or sites are safe for AI grounding?		
Operational	Do we have clear governance, monitoring, and incident response processes for AI?		
Cultural	Do our people understand AI enough to use it responsibly?		

Instructions

1. For each domain, rate your organization's readiness from 1 (low) to 5 (high).
2. Discuss what evidence supports your score.
3. Identify the top two areas that need improvement.

4. Assign owners and timelines for specific next steps.
    - You can repeat this exercise quarterly to measure progress and keep the conversation active.

From Risk to Readiness

Risk should not be seen as a blocker to innovation. It is the foundation of responsible experimentation. When you gauge your readiness through the lens of data, operational, and cultural risk, you are not slowing progress. Instead, you are ensuring that progress lasts and you are helping to avoid any surprises that might otherwise derail your efforts. Throughout my career, I have run into many situations where project teams attempted to circumvent the necessary Legal, Compliance, and Risk buy-in, which ultimately ended up not only slowing down their efforts but, in some situations, stopping the project altogether.

In the IGNITE framework, this phase is about awareness and balance. You are not yet deploying at scale, but you are laying the groundwork for confidence. The organization that understands its risk landscape will move faster later because it will not be constantly reacting to surprises. Additionally, this is a core aspect of change management in that you are informing a set of stakeholders about your plans and then hearing and responding to their concerns.

Before moving into the next phase, take a moment to ask yourself and your leadership team three questions:

1. Have we identified where our greatest AI risks live?
2. Are our people prepared to manage those risks confidently?
3. Do we have a shared understanding of what "acceptable risk" means for our business?

Once you can answer yes, you have successfully gauged your readiness. You are ready to move forward to the next phase of IGNITE, where risk management evolves into Nurturing Guardrails and scaling AI responsibly becomes part of your organizational DNA.

Key Takeaways

Gauging readiness is about honesty, not optimism. It means confronting the realities of your data, operations, and culture before chasing the excitement of AI at scale. Organizations that invest time here build a stronger foundation of trust and control, turning potential risks into strategic advantages. In the next chapter, we'll focus on Nail Pilots and how to design small, high-impact experiments that prove real value and prepare your organization to scale AI responsibly.

CHAPTER 4

Nail Pilots

Are we trying to stack the deck in favor of a certain outcome, or are we genuinely testing whether there's real value?

—Nancy Davis
Former Vice President and Chief Information Officer at Pratt & Whitney

From Hype to Evidence

The Gauge stage told you where the landmines are across data, operations, and organizational culture. Now, it is time to pick a safe, high-value spot to plant your first flag. Nail Pilots is about choosing two or three use cases that are small enough to run fast yet big enough to prove that AI can move the needle. You will decide whether a pre-built copilot, a bespoke agent, or some other solution will provide you with the quickest path to value. You will need to frame each pilot with a clear goal, success metric, and exit criterion. The result is a short list your sponsor can fund tomorrow, and your change team can launch next Monday.

In this chapter, we will take you through the lifecycle of first defining the purpose of the pilot, then selecting the right use cases, building your pilot playbook to help ensure you are able to measure impact, and avoiding some of the common pitfalls that tend to occur with this phase of most AI transformations. These pilots are also your opportunity to test governance

J. Matfess, *Your New Colleague is a Copilot*, Inside Copilot,
https://doi.org/10.1007/979-8-8688-2619-1_4

guardrails in a controlled environment before scaling them enterprise-wide. The insights gathered here will shape not just future use cases but the playbook your organization uses to manage risk and growth in parallel.

Define the Purpose of Your Pilot

Before you even start to entertain cloud platforms, LLMs, or even the specific use cases themselves, you really should start with defining the purpose of your pilot. If your purpose is to "kick the tires" of a particular technical solution, then you are already setting yourself up for a potential failure. The purpose of your AI pilot should not be aligned solely to technical feasibility but rather should be tied to a specific business outcome that you are trying to drive. It might seem nuanced, but it's a huge difference to plan for "technically validating Microsoft 365 Copilot to see how it works," compared to "let's see how Microsoft 365 Copilot can help our social media team respond more efficiently to customer concerns."

Often, I have worked with customers that have started with "IT Pilots" of a specific technology, only to see those efforts never leave the evaluation phase. There are a number of reasons for these pilots getting stalled out, including sometimes IT is not as intimate with the business processes as they thought they were, or they didn't have a well-structured exit criteria defined for the pilot. The value of bringing the business into your pilots is they are the owners of the processes that you are attempting to optimize. They will understand the various nuances associated with those processes and the steps that are manual or require often rework, and they also can help co-create the success criteria that are needed to evaluate if the pilot was successful or not.

Balancing Pilot vs. Production

Building upon what we learned in the previous chapter, there are many risk considerations when it comes to AI. When you embark on your pilot, you must also carefully balance the need to enable your pilot with the effort that it might take to scale from Pilot to Production. IT Security Professionals tend to err on the side of caution, knowing that an exciting IT pilot can immediately become something that the CEO or COO would like to promote to Production sooner than later. This C-Suite visibility tends to put additional pressure on an already overworked area of the business; therefore, you should anticipate some level of pushback for any requests to reduce or minimize the security requirements for your project. What may seem like a "small pilot" can be viewed as a high-risk activity by those who have lived through the rapid "Pilot-to-Production" requests from the C-Suite.

There are a couple of ways to address this potential friction with your IT security team, including having the Pilot to Production conversation early. It's important to capture their requirements and try to establish a road map for when certain elements need to be in place. The goal is to clearly understand what is needed to support the Pilot activity, and then what might be considered Production readiness requirements. While the tasks themselves may be similar, sometimes the robustness of those solutions may not be. For example, your IT Security team may request that all human-to-AI interactions be logged to a database that they can monitor.

For a pilot, you may be able to negotiate a logging solution that is temporary vs. integrating logging activities into your enterprise Security Incident and Event Management ("SIEM") platform. Other IT Security teams, however, may view this step as a prerequisite before approving your solution for production. I have found that including IT Security early in your project is actually a benefit rather than a deterrent. Even more ideal is to ensure that there is some representation from IT Security Leadership as a stakeholder in your project. This can help not only navigate the various security requirements you are being tasked with, but it may also help prioritize the review and approval of your pilot by the assigned IT Security representative.

You Don't Know What You Don't Know!

It might sound a little bit awkward, but it's okay to be vulnerable about what you don't know. Often, technical professionals assume that they need to have everything figured out before embarking on a pilot, but that's not true. In addition to validating a particular business outcome, your pilot plan should also include learning elements. Basically, what are the things that you hope to learn through this effort. To do this well will require you to assume some level of vulnerability in that you are openly acknowledging that there are things that you do not know going into the pilot. I have found that business professionals tend to get uncomfortable with being vulnerable in the workplace; however, this should be considered a strength and not a weakness.

Surprisingly, when you speak with executives, they tend to appreciate when employees are open and honest with them. It helps them lower their own defensive walls and makes for a tighter partnership. Part of their role as executive sponsors is to help ensure you are taking a holistic view of your pilot and not introducing any unplanned risk. Communicating what you perhaps "don't know" in advance of your pilot is helpful; however, you should also consider communicating any hypotheses that you hope to prove out, which can be inclusive of business outcomes, security, and governance design decisions. Now that we have worked through some of the guardrails for your pilot, let's go ahead and step through identifying the right use cases for your AI pilot.

SELECTING THE RIGHT PILOT USE CASES

Selecting the right pilot use cases is one of the most fun and challenging aspects of any AI project. The goal is to balance use cases that are both high-impact and low-risk. This careful balance is what will help to ensure that your pilot does not get bogged down in legal, compliance, or internal politics. Every organization is different; therefore, it is challenging to be prescriptive as to exactly what will trigger different parts of your organization to have a reaction to your pilot. We are going to build off the initial brainstorming from Chapter 1 and get very specific with the business outcomes this use case will drive, the individuals impacted, and what's needed to make it a success.

For this exercise, follow each of the steps with your project team to ensure that you have not only confirmed the appropriate use case, datasets, and action items, but also try to preemptively identify any risks or challenges that might negatively impact your project schedule.

Step 1: Define the High-level Use Case

First, in your team, you'll want to talk through your use case collectively to make sure that there is a common understanding of what problem you are attempting to solve. Use Table 4-1 as a guide to navigating this conversation, and capture your responses.

Table 4-1. High-Level Use Case Details

Question	Example Answer	Your Answer
What's the intended outcome of your pilot?	Summarize and extract key actions from project updates	
Who would be the target persona or role within the organization that would benefit from this use case?	Project managers, project coordinators, and business analysts who prepare these reports.	
What specific repetitive or manual task could AI help with?	Capturing meeting minutes, drafting meeting agendas, or creating status reports.	

Step 2: Identify Candidate Data Sources

Next, you will want to identify and list up to five unstructured data sources that may support your use case. Examples: Microsoft Teams Channels, departmental SharePoint sites, Google Drives, shared OneDrive folders, or document libraries, as outlined in Table 4-2.

Table 4-2. Inventorying Your Unstructured Data Sources

Data Source	Description	Owner/Steward	Location
HR Policy Library	Contains policies, templates, and historical versions	HR Operations	SharePoint
Contact Center Conversation Transcripts	Meeting notes and customer escalations	Contact Center Reps	OneDrive

Step 3: Score Each Dataset

After inventory, what you will want to do is rate each dataset from **1 (low)** to **5 (high)** across ten readiness criteria. This is helpful to validate that the dataset you're targeting will help you achieve the necessary business outcome. This is also meant to help identify any potential blockers, red flags, or issues to remediate before moving forward with including that dataset into your AI pilot. You should encourage some spirited conversation and justification among your project team members to ensure that no one voice is speaking over others. You can capture your scores as shown in Table 4-3, and then tally up your scores to help confirm the viability of this use case.

Table 4-3. *High-Level Use Case Details*

Criteria	Key Question	Score (1–5)
Relevance	Summarize and extract key actions from project updates.	
Accessibility	Can authorized users and AI services access the data easily?	
Quality	Are files readable, well-named, and relatively current?	
Sensitivity	Does it contain minimal personal or confidential information?	
Volume and Variety	Is there enough data (hundreds or thousands of items) to show useful patterns?	
Ownership	Is there a clear owner who can approve the data source for AI use?	

(continued)

Table 4-3. (*continued*)

Criteria	Key Question	Score (1–5)
Traceability	Can outputs be verified against the original sources?	
Change Frequency	Is the content relatively stable (not constantly overwritten)?	
Business Value	Would using this data create measurable time savings or insight?	
Compliance Fit	Does it align with company data handling and AI policies?	

Total Score: _____ / 50
Interpretation:

- **41–50:** Excellent candidate for a GenAI pilot
- **26–40:** Possibly viable with cleanup or redaction
- **0–25:** High risk or low value—defer for later

Step 4: Plan Next Actions

After confirming the viability, you will need to start assigning action items to the project team to help validate the datasets with the data owners to be able to progress forward with your pilot. You should capture both owners and due dates as shown in Table 4-4.

Table 4-4. Assigning Action Items and Next Steps

Action Item	Owner	Due Date
Confirm data owner approval		
Define pilot data scope (e.g., one document library, site, set of pages)		
Review document and page permissions		
Perform remediation if required		
Prepare a pilot dataset sample		

Reference: Red Flags in Unstructured Data

Table 4-5 is meant to serve as a quick gut-check as you evaluate data sources for each use case. Use it to spot red flags that will slow you down or introduce risk and to prioritize sources that are structured, current, and safe for AI to learn from. If your content leans heavily into the red flags, pause and fix those issues before you label anything as AI-ready. If most of your sources align with the positive indicators, you are in a strong position to move forward with pilots that are both useful and defensible.

Table 4-5. Red Flags and Positive Indicators

⚠ Red Flags	✅ Positive Indicators
Contains Personally Identifiable Information ("PII"), Personal Health Information ("PHI"), or confidential financial info	Primarily business process documents or knowledge artifacts
Outdated or duplicated files	Current, version-controlled materials
Chat transcripts with personal data of clients, customers, or employees	Clearly structured folders and labeled documents

The "Pilot Playbook"

The pilot playbook is where you move from abstract enthusiasm about AI to a concrete, accountable plan. Your playbook needs to spell out who owns what, how success will be measured, and what must be true before you trust this thing with real people and real data. Some example roles to prioritize are an executive sponsor who removes blockers and reinforces the "why," a maker or build team who owns configuration and iteration, a data owner who is responsible for what the pilot can see, and your IT and security partners who validate that you are not trading speed for risk.

Next, define success in plain language before a single user touches the solution. Are you trying to improve customer experience through hyper-personalization, increase self-service, reduce time spent on a particular task or process, or deflect tickets from a help desk queue? Pick a small set of measurable outcomes, such as "80% of responses rated helpful," "30% reduction in time to complete this task," or "X hours saved per week for this team." If the metric does not map to a real business outcome or a real behavior change, it does not belong in your pilot.

Also, no pilot should go live without passing a simple governance checklist. Confirm the agent or solutions can only see what they should see, validate permissions and sharing, and remove obviously risky locations from scope. Verify that the data is current enough to be useful and not cluttered with junk that will confuse responses. Work with your IT Security team to identify any other tasks that will help further reduce their anxiety with your pilot and improve the posture should this need to scale to Production at some point. When a governance checklist in your AI experiments becomes the norm, pilots stop being scary experiments and start becoming safe, repeatable patterns your organization can trust. It not only gives you the lead for these efforts' credibility, but it also serves as a model that others can and should follow to replicate your success.

Finally, your pilot also needs a deliberate feedback loop, not a vague "tell us what you think." Combine qualitative input (what users loved, what felt confusing, where it broke trust) with quantitative signals (usage, frequency, accuracy ratings, escalation rates). Make it easy for people to respond: a built-in rating prompt, a short recurring survey, a quick huddle with pilot users. The goal is to treat feedback as fuel for improvement, not as a compliance exercise. Also, recognize that not everyone provides feedback in the same way, and there may be personas that would prefer to share this feedback in-person vs. through a form. Meeting your users where they are is vital to ensuring that you have a true measure as to how things are progressing. Building off the topic of collecting feedback, let's talk about measuring impact.

Measuring Impact

As mentioned before, the role of IT is not to play with the new "bright shiny object" but to help solve real business problems with technology. To help justify the investments in technology, you need to be able to measure the impact of your investment. Qualitative and quantitative measures are two types of evaluation metrics (or assessment methods) used when measuring impact. Quantitative measures capture numerical data, which are things that you can count or calculate. Some examples include usage rates, time saved, or cost reduction. Table 4-6 provides an example of how you can approach tracking quantitative impact of your solution.

Table 4-6. *Example Quantitative Measure Capture*

Persona	Full-Time Rate	Usage Metrics	Time Savings	Quantitative Impact
Project Manager	$60/hour	3x/day	5 hours/month	$300/month
Finance Analyst	$58/hour	4x/day	4 hours/month	$232/month
HR Specialist	$45/hour	5x/day	6 hours/month	$270/month
Marketing Coordinator	$35/hour	8x/day	8 hours/month	$280/month

Qualitative measures, on the other hand, capture perceptions, experiences, and context. Basically, these are things you can describe, such as user satisfaction, cultural change, or confidence levels, which are more subjective. Some measures for you to consider include

- **Quality Improvement** - Captures how AI changed the standard or consistency of their work.
- **Ease of Work** - Reflects perceived effort, clarity, or flow in daily tasks.
- **Confidence in AI Output** - Gauges how much trust users place in AI-generated results.
- **Overall Job Satisfaction** - Measures emotional response and engagement after adoption.

You should then plan to capture the qualitative measures and share the results with your stakeholders, using Table 4-7 as a reference for potentially how to lay that data out.

Table 4-7. *Example Qualitative Measurements*

Persona	Quality Improvement	Ease of Work	Confidence in AI Output	Overall Job Satisfaction
Project Manager	Fewer errors and clearer project summaries	Work feels more organized and predictable	Growing trust in results	↑ Moderate; workdays feel less chaotic
Finance Analyst	More consistent reconciliations and reporting accuracy	Repetitive tasks feel easier	Moderate confidence, improving over time	↑ Moderate; less stress at month-end
HR Specialist	Better communication drafts and templates	Workflows feel smoother and more human	High confidence in responses	↑ Significant; more time for strategic work
Marketing Coordinator	More consistent brand tone and creative variety	Feels more creative and in control	Very high, often uses AI first	↑ Strong; renewed enthusiasm for projects

Together, your quantitative and qualitative measures form a balanced way to evaluate impact. They help to combine "what happened" with "why it mattered." Use cases will differ in terms of how easily you can measure these two types of metrics. For solutions targeting knowledge workers whose day will tend to vary greatly, it might be necessary to lean more into the qualitative measurements since their work may not be as predictable or repeatable. On the other hand, where you have very well-defined and repeatable processes with historic benchmarks such as average call time, quantitative measurements will be your best friend. Another complementary measurement is the lessons learned from your pilot.

Document Learnings and Share Outcomes

Investing in a pilot is more than just proving out technology and modeling potential future state processes. Part of the value in your investment is what you learn along the way. This is particularly evident in the field of AI, which is progressing at an exceptionally rapid pace in terms of technological innovation. Learning can come in many forms, such as

- What worked technically
- What policies or procedures may need to be updated
- What didn't work as expected
- How did users engage with the technology vs how we thought they might engage

As a reminder, it's not good enough for just the project team to be aware of these findings. You need to share findings with other teams, including your executive leaders, your AI Steering Committee or AI Office, and other business and technology teams that may also be piloting AI. There is a good chance that your findings can help others who may be embarking on this same journey. Sharing helps promote a culture of learning and may also help turn the page around after failure. We'll delve into the concept of failure during pilots in more detail in Chapter 5.

Common Pitfalls

Not all pilots succeed, and that's a good thing. However, certain conditions within your control should be addressed to help mitigate the potential risk of failure. Some of these include

- **Avoiding Overengineering the Pilot** – The goal should never be to prove out every feature/function of an AI solution. The more technical integrations and technical capabilities will introduce complexities that might deviate from solving business problems.

- **No Executive Sponsor** - Executive sponsorship is key for ensuring that you receive the necessary organizational support to conduct your pilot. Executives have the power to remove blockers, prioritize individuals' assistance, and ultimately will be the decision-makers when it comes to deciding whether a pilot should be scaled to production.
- **Not Defining Exit Criteria** - Pilots often lack clear end points, resulting in no defined completion or "definition of done." You should ensure that your pilot is not one of the many others that linger around long after they should.
- **Piloting Without IT Security and Compliance Support** - The potential organizational risk surrounding AI warrants that you include those responsible for managing risk and compliance as part of your pilot. Ideally, you will have representation from these teams on your project team, but if that isn't possible, at a minimum, you should ensure that they are considered key stakeholders for your pilot.

This list is not exhaustive of every potential pitfall, but it should hopefully serve as a reminder to consider the full lifecycle of starting and ending your pilot so that you can move on to the next one.

Key Takeaways

Successful pilots are built on clarity of purpose, measurable outcomes, and active feedback loops. The goal is not to prove that AI works in general, but to demonstrate where it creates real value for your people and processes. A balanced mix of qualitative and quantitative measures ensures you capture both the efficiency gains and the human experience behind them. When pilots are well-scoped, governed, and openly shared, they evolve from experiments into repeatable models your organization can trust. In the next chapter, we'll focus on the Iterate phase and how to adopt an Agile mindset to AI.

CHAPTER 5

Iterate

Move fast and break things. Unless you are breaking stuff, you are not moving fast enough.

—Mark Zuckerberg
Founder, Chairman, and Chief Executive Officer (CEO) of Meta Platforms, Inc.

Move Fast and Break Things

You have inspired people to care about AI, and you have built a business case that leadership can stand behind. You have gauged your readiness across data, operations, and culture so that you are not walking into risk with your eyes closed. You have selected pilots that are meaningful, responsible, and positioned to win. This is the stage of IGNITE where you stop talking about AI's potential and start proving it. It is not glamorous, and it is not something that belongs on a keynote stage. It is a working session in a conference room at 4:30 p.m. on a Friday, with a half-finished cold coffee, a disheveled whiteboard, and three people trying to decide whether this agent is helping anyone.

Handled well, Iterate is your engine for creating momentum and driving progress forward. It creates a loop of building, testing, listening, and improving that keeps your pilots honest and your stakeholders engaged. Handled poorly, it turns into "that AI thing" that everyone

J. Matfess, *Your New Colleague is a Copilot*, Inside Copilot,
https://doi.org/10.1007/979-8-8688-2619-1_5

stops believing in. This chapter will show you how to design iteration as a deliberate practice, not an accident. It will feel familiar in structure and tone if you have come through the earlier chapters: practical, grounded, and focused on the challenges that organizations face.

Building a Team That Can Iterate Together!

So, before we even get into the nuts and bolts of iteration, let's talk about the foundation: building a true team. Iteration is not just about process or tech; it's about getting everyone genuinely on the same page. That means you've got to form a team that trusts each other, one that knows from the start: we win as a team, and if we stumble, we stumble as a team. It's that collective mindset that lays the groundwork for everything else and allows you to work together to drive forward in the same direction.

Now, building that trust takes a bit of intentional effort. It's not just about work tasks; it's about sharing a bit about yourselves, learning how each person ticks, and figuring out everyone's preferred way of working. Maybe someone's all about in-person huddles, maybe someone else has evening commitments and needs a little flexibility. Whatever it is, understanding your teammates as individuals, not just by their job titles, is how you turn a group of individuals into a well-oiled machine. As humans, we tend to fear the unknown. However, by getting to know the people behind the title, we can start to feel more comfortable interacting with them. And this demystifying of those individuals is the starting point for building trust that fuels high-performing teams.

And let's not forget the elephant in the room: conflict. Healthy conflict is a powerhouse for growth, but only if you've agreed on how to handle it. You want to hash out upfront how you'll address disagreements, so they don't turn into finger-pointing or morale killers. This may be particularly challenging in company cultures that are not accustomed to managing conflict effectively. Growing up in an aerospace and defense culture,

I struggled at times when adjusting to company cultures that were more mature in managing conflict. The value of addressing how to manage conflict is necessary, because when everyone feels safe to speak up and knows that disagreements are just part of the process, iteration becomes significantly smoother.

So, before you even start iterating or thinking about failing fast, you need to ensure that your team is rock-solid. That's how you create a space where everyone's aligned, everyone's comfortable pivoting, and everyone's ready to tackle the next challenge together. Now, let's step through an exercise that can be used to help you begin to develop and build your team.

BUILDING A TEAM THAT CAN ITERATE

Now, to put all of this into practice, here's a simple activity you can run with your team. Think of it as your "Team Charter and Conflict Compass" exercise: it's going to help you set the stage for trust and give you a framework for dealing with disagreements before they get thorny.

Team Charter and Conflict Compass Exercise

1. **Set the Stage (10 minutes) –** Gather everyone together, either virtually or in person. And explain that the goal is to co-create a team charter. This is where you'll all agree on how you want to work together and how you'll handle bumps in the road.

2. **Share and Listen (15 minutes) –** Have each team member share a little about their working style and any personal preferences—do they prefer morning meetings or afternoon check-ins? Are there certain days they have other commitments? This helps everyone get a feel for each other as people, not just roles.

3. **Draft the Charter (15 minutes)** – As a group, write down a few key agreements. How often will you check in? How will you celebrate wins or handle feedback? This becomes your team's mini playbook.
4. **Conflict Compass (10 minutes)** – Finally, agree on a simple method for resolving conflicts. Maybe it's a quick "pause and discuss" rule or a commitment to assume positive intent before jumping to conclusions. Whatever it is, get everyone to buy in so you have a shared way to keep things smooth.

By the end of this exercise, you'll have not just a team, but a team that's ready to iterate together, handle whatever comes their way, and fail fast without fear.

Why Waterfall Doesn't Work for AI

Let's get this out of the way early: AI moves too fast for the waterfall project management methodology. If you aren't quite sure what I'm talking about, waterfall project management is a linear, sequential approach to project management. Waterfall projects progress through distinct phases, with each phase requiring completion before the next one can begin. The typical phases include requirements gathering, design, development, testing, deployment, and finally maintenance. Once a phase is finished, teams rarely go back to make changes.

When it comes to an AI project, you can't spec out a solution for six months, build it for six more, then hand it off for user acceptance testing and hope it lands. That methodology assumes fixed business and technical requirements. AI, on the other hand, is shifting under your feet in almost real-time. Additionally, since it's evolving rapidly and people are just beginning to learn it, your users won't know what they genuinely want until they start interacting with it. Your stakeholders will see one demo and change the scope. And your security and compliance teams will continue to layer in new guardrails as GenAI capabilities evolve. That's not a bug; that's the nature of innovation in a fast-paced AI-enabled world.

So instead of resisting that change, we embrace it. We build in short sprints, get honest feedback early, and adapt as we go. Much of this work involves embracing the chaos and being prepared for rapid change. You shouldn't set an expectation that you will get things perfect the first time. Rather, you should set the expectations that you will make incremental progress, gain feedback, and then work to adjust based on what you have learned. To help drive this iteration, you'll need to focus on the "success criteria," which we will explore next.

Success Criteria: Not "Done," but "Useful"

In traditional Agile projects, the end of a sprint signifies that a body of work is considered "done." This typically refers to features or functions being configured, developed, or modified. In AI pilots, we need to redefine the definition of done slightly. In AI pilots, "done" doesn't mean perfect; it means *useful*. Are we realizing value from what we have built, and is it something that we can continue to work with while the technology and requirements evolve based on the output?

At the end of each sprint, you want a tangible artifact. This can be a functioning workflow, a prototype, or a piece of functionality within an AI agent that performs a specific task. But more importantly, you want something that solicits meaningful feedback from your business users. The point of each iteration is to validate whether you're solving the *right* problem the *right* way.

Here's how to frame it:

- **Start with the "Why"** - Remind stakeholders of the problem you're solving and why it matters.
- **Show What Changed** - Walk through what you built or improved in this iteration.
- **Capture the Reaction** - Don't just ask *"do you like it?"* You also need to ask, "would you use this today?"

Success isn't shipping code. It's shipping confidence.

Designing Your Feedback Rituals

If you want to iterate fast, you need feedback that is honest, structured, and predictable. Most AI pilots do not fall apart because the technology failed. They fall apart because the team did not create a steady rhythm of listening. Feedback cannot be something you collect only when someone remembers to send a message; it needs to be incorporated into your project team's rhythm of interacting with their business. stakeholders

The best teams set up a feedback cadence the same way they set up sprint planning. It can be a weekly 30-minute session where users walk through what worked, what felt clunky, and what they would never use in real life. It can be a written form that captures examples of both helpful and unhelpful responses, which your team can review during the next sprint. The most important thing is that the ritual is consistent. When feedback has a home, people are more willing to share it, and your team is more equipped to act on it.

Once you establish that rhythm, your iteration cycles become more predictable. You can see patterns instead of isolated opinions. You can tell if a prompt issue is an edge case or a real flaw. You can identify where the user experience is breaking down long before your pilot loses credibility. That is the work that keeps your iteration steady and your pilots alive.

But what are we iterating on? Let's talk about that next!

What to Technically Iterate On?

When you're figuring out what exactly to iterate on in your AI projects, think of it like a three-legged stool. The first leg is the large language models themselves, the GPT-5s, Claudes, and Geminis. Not every large language model will be a perfect fit for every job. Each one of these models has its own personality, strengths, and weaknesses. Therefore, part of iterating is asking: is this model the right dance partner, or should we swap it out and see if another one waltzes a little better? This is likely where you will need to consult with the Data Scientists or Data Engineers on your project team to help understand which model might be the best fit for your use case. They may leverage some of the open-source benchmarking sites, such as Live Bench (`https://livebench.ai`), to help provide recommendations for any model changes that might be necessary for your use case.

Next up are the prompts, either the ones that your users send to the models or the system instructions that you provide for grounding the responses. Prompts are your secret sauce, your magic spell, and your programming language for AI. Words matter a ton, and the nuances of language are impactful enough to have a measurable impact on how your model supports a use case. Another iteration is tweaking how you communicate with your model, refining those prompts until the AI provides you with a helpful response. Like other programming efforts, this iteration can take several attempts before you get it just right.

Then, there's the data. If your use case feels off, maybe it's a data problem. Sometimes, you need to curate more relevant information, fine-tune it with better examples, or provide the right context if you're using a retrieval-augmented approach. For example, consider a use case where you are providing policies and procedures for your organization. If you find yourself receiving responses that reference outdated policies, you likely have a data problem that needs to be addressed. You will need to work with your data owners to purge that obsolete data, either through deletion or archival.

Iteration is not only about what happens inside the model or the data pipeline. It also depends on how people experience the solution in their day-to-day work. The way the application feels, responds, and guides users has a direct impact on whether your pilot gains momentum or stalls. With that in mind, let's take a closer look at the role of user experience in your iteration cycles.

User Experience As an Iteration

When people think about iteration in AI, they naturally jump to the model, the prompts, or the data. Those are important, but they are not what your users notice first. Most of the time, a pilot gains or loses momentum because the experience feels either smooth or frustrating. User experience becomes one of your strongest signals for determining whether the iteration is working or not.

AI introduces a different type of user interaction. People are not clicking through a series of screens or following a fixed process. They are either talking or typing to something that feels very conversational. Typically, they expect that conversation to be fast, accurate, and easy. However, when that flow is disrupted, users will interpret the whole solution as broken. And it doesn't even have to be broken or throw an error message. A disruption to a user experience can be as simple as friction in data entry.

An example of this can be seen in Figure 5-1, where a user interacts with a "Task Tracker" agent. This agent offers a straightforward experience that allows you to leverage it to submit tasks to a Microsoft To-Do list. It leverages Microsoft's Power Platform connectors to integrate an AI agent with the Microsoft To-Do service. The friction that the user will experience is when assigning a date for when the task can be completed.

The experience using the To-Do Tool is that the input it is expecting for the due date is in the format of "YYYY-MM-DDThh:mm:ss", which is not very natural for the user. You cannot, by default, provide the date as a string, such as "September 9, 2026".

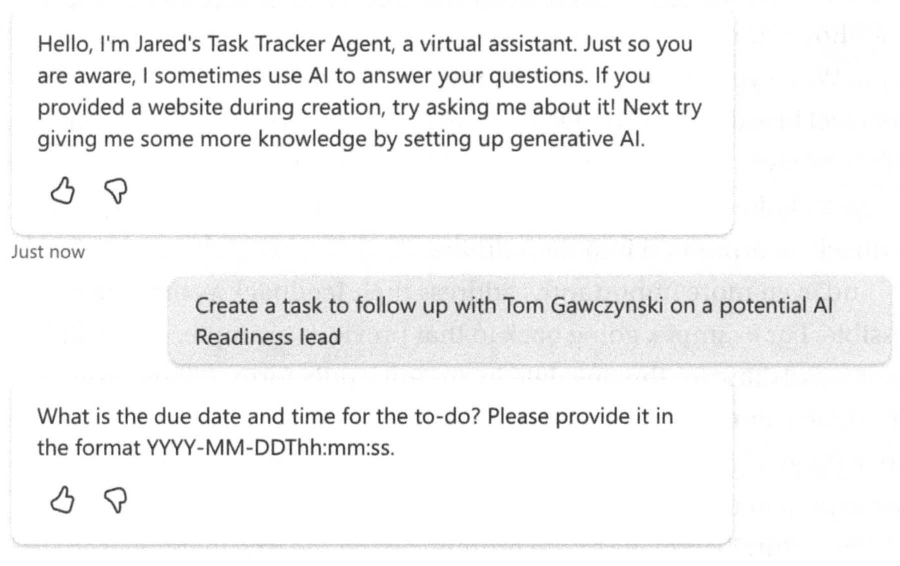

Figure 5-1. *A Task Tracker Agent Prompting a User for a Due Date*

As you run your pilots, listen for the minor signs of friction that your users may be experiencing with your solution. This could be like the previous example, where the input for a due date is not very intuitive and would require the user to pull up their phone, calendar, or another application to complete. There are other examples of where a user might provide feedback about a negative experience, such as waiting too long for a response or receiving a perceived incorrect response. Or the agent may request the same piece of information twice. The prompt to get started may be unclear, or the instructions may be too technical. These small gaps add up. They can sink something that is technically excellent but practically awkward.

To catch these issues early, sit with your users while they work. Watch how they move through the experience, where their eyes go, how many steps it takes to get an answer, and what they do when they feel stuck. Remember to pay attention to what they mutter under their breath or the questions they ask each other. These moments reveal a great deal more about how your users perceive your solution than an electronic survey ever could. When you do catch these moments, you should ensure that your users feel heard. Acknowledge their feedback, and then, after you have had time to analyze the effort to make modifications to improve the experience, be sure to follow up with them on when they should expect to see their feedback incorporated into the solution.

And even more importantly, address their feedback as timely as possible. For example, going back to that previous example, where the agent was asking for the due date in an unfriendly format. If the user experience for this solution is meant to be chat-based, presenting the user with a lightweight form within the chat window may prove to be a better user experience.

The natural language or the prompt can be the way that the user invokes the agent to go ahead and log the task. However, the actual collection of that information can be presented as a lightweight form, as pictured in Figure 5-2. This would allow the user to leverage a date picker control to select the due date vs. trying to mentally navigate a calendar.

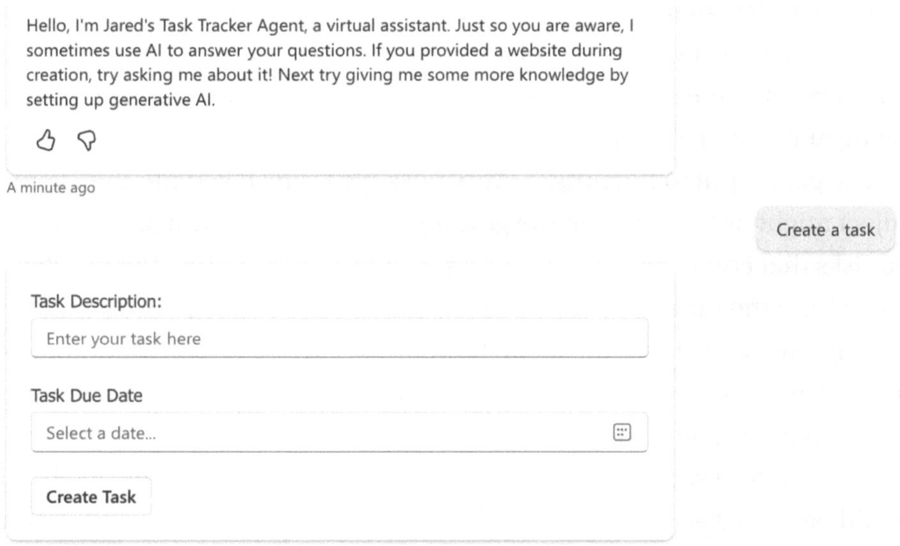

Figure 5-2. *A Task Tracker Agent with a Date Picker*

For a simple approach, focus on the points where users tend to hesitate. Hesitation is the honest indicator of friction for your users. When you identify these moments, you can shape your next iteration around resolving them. When the experience is smooth, intuitive, and predictable, your users will treat the agent as something that fits naturally into their work rather than something they need to fight with. That is a significant win for any AI pilot and is something that you should track for impact, as we'll discuss further in Chapter 6.

Creating a Project Risk Log

Every iteration introduces new risks to your project. Some of these risks are technical, some are operational, and some are political. If you do not track them, your team will discover them at the worst possible moment, usually during a stakeholder review. A simple project risk log provides visibility into potential issues before they become a roadblock. While this is a standard project deliverable for most project management methodologies, it isn't always leveraged as a tool to navigate risk. Instead, it's often viewed as a chore, or something that you must do to check the box for your Project Management Office's requirements.

The goal is not to document every possible issue; if you did that, your project might not ever get off the ground. The goal is to surface the one or two risks that could stall your progress. Maybe you're getting inconsistent results from the model, or the connectors that you're using are not pulling the right line of business data. Maybe your user group is not responding to feedback requests, or their feedback is mixed or unhelpful. Perhaps your security team is about to implement a new control that impacts your data sources. Capture each one of these risks in your Project Risk Log. Each risk should have an assigned owner and a status. The owner of that risk should then take the lead to try and identify a mitigation step to try, ideally before the next sprint.

It's not just about having a risk log; it's important that you incorporate it into your project ceremonies. Ideally, you should be reviewing this log weekly, to keep your team aligned and your leadership informed. It also reduces stress because you are not hiding problems or scrambling to explain them afterward. You are showing that your project delivery is controlled, responsible, and transparent. That is the kind of signal that builds confidence and secures long-term support from your executive stakeholders. While the concept of managing a project risk log is not unique to AI, I have found that these projects are inherently more risky than the ones that have been replicated multiple times before. There isn't an infinite playbook to draw from, so managing these risks well will be helpful for ensuring project success.

How to Fail Fast?

So, here's the thing: on paper, "fail fast" sounds like a no-brainer. It's logical, it's even friendly on the ears. But when you're the one steering the pilot, and you realize, "Hey, we might need to let this thing flop on purpose," that's when it gets real. You start second-guessing: is it me? Do I not get it? Are we missing some secret ingredient here? That is a tough spot to be in, especially if you are someone who finds joy in solving problems. I recall working on a firewall change many years ago that ultimately broke our contractor extranet solution. Instead of rolling back the change, the team implementing it spent the next 10+ hours continuing to troubleshoot and adjust the configuration. They kept dozens of testers up throughout the evening, eventually fixing the issue a half hour into the first shift for our warehouse contractors.

As you can see from that story, overcoming failure is not always something that comes naturally to technical professionals. In my example, the impact was not catastrophic. The first shift was able to make up for the lost time, and the testers caught up on sleep. Still, it was a clear lesson in how IT teams sometimes chase heroics instead of following basic ITIL principles of rolling back changes when they fail. That instinct to push through is common, often stemming from pride, skill, and the belief that we can troubleshoot our way out of any problem. It can also make it harder to accept when a pilot needs to be paused or reshaped rather than rescued.

When it comes to AI, sometimes you need to back off because the technology isn't there yet, or the model isn't ready, or perhaps the use case is just too large and needs to be broken down into smaller chunks. The point is that failing fast is essential when dealing with a rapidly evolving space, such as AI. It shows you where the boundaries are, helps you reshape the problem, and lets you pivot toward something doable. So, ideally, you should try to embrace it, learn from it, and let it guide you to the next iteration. And sometimes you should say, this isn't quite working and we may need to recalibrate how we are approaching this problem. This also means informing your stakeholders about the new direction you think you are taking.

Executive Stakeholder Support

Now, here's the kicker for failing fast: To make this work, you need your leadership on board from the get-go. They've got to get that a pilot is an experiment, and sometimes experiments just don't hit the bullseye. By setting that expectation up front, you help to prepare them for the fast-moving nature of AI, to the fact that many of us are still learning together. It also helps reinforce the learning aspect of a pilot that collectively you do in fact have going in hypotheses, but that the role of the team is to explore objectively. By setting this expectation upfront, you're giving yourself room to pivot without drama. It's all about that transparency, keeping them in the loop on what you're seeing, and why you're making a call to either shift gears or scale down the use case.

In other words, the secret sauce to failing fast isn't just about you or your team. The secret sauce is making sure your leadership is nodding along and saying, "Yep, we expected some of these trials not to pan out." That way, when you pull the plug on a direction that's not working, it's not a failure. Instead, it's just an informed step toward finding what will work next. And that next might, in fact, be a recommendation to scale beyond the pilot, either to recruit additional users to provide their input as well. Alternatively, it may be that the findings from your pilot have proven sufficient value, making it worthwhile to consider what this might look like at the full scale of your organization. Let's step through an exercise to help with performing that evaluation.

EXERCISE: TWEAK, REPLACE, KILL, OR SCALE?

Before you scale anything, you need to make one tough call: Is this pilot worth more of your team's time? Iteration isn't just about tweaking; it's about knowing when to walk away, when to reinvest, and when to burn it down. This exercise will help you and your team put real structure around that decision so it's not just a gut feeling. This exercise is intended to be conducted with both your project team members and one to two representatives from the business. It can be done either virtually or in-person, and try to carve out about 30–60 minutes, depending on the size of the team and complexity of the use case.

Step 1: Score the Pilot Across Four Dimensions *(10 Minutes)*

The first step is to solicit input from your business users, using a 1-5 scale. You should consider 1 to mean the solution provides a very low value for that criterion, and 5 if it provides a high level of value. The intent is to have them rate your pilot use case and the features or functionality delivered across the following criteria, as shown in Table 5-1.

Table 5-1. *High-level Use Case Details*

Dimension	Question	Score (1–5)
Value	Has the solution started to solve a meaningful business problem?	
Usability	Are users adopting it with minimal friction?	
Accuracy	Is it delivering trustworthy, helpful results?	
Feedback Loop	Do we have a mechanism to provide feedback and improve the functionality?	

Add up your scores (Max: 20).

Step 2: Apply the Matrix *(5 Minutes)*

Your next step as a team is to review the scoring matrix shown in Table 5-2 and capture any conversations among the team. The intent is not to reconsider changing scores, but rather to confirm that the scores are accurate.

Table 5-2. *Scoring Value Matrix*

Total Score	Decision	Comments
16–20	**Scale** – The pilot is ready for broader rollout. Invest in expanding adoption	
11–15	**Tweak** – Your pilot has promise. Consider refining the prompts, updating the data sources, or modifying the user experience based on feedback.	
6–10	**Replace** – The core idea or use case might be right, but the current approach isn't. Consider a different user experience, model, or overall method to satisfy this use case.	
0–5	**Kill** – Despite your best intentions, this isn't working. Perform a lesson learned exercise, and free up team capacity for other efforts.	

Step 3: Reflection Exercise *(5–10 Minutes)*

Finally, everyone should take a few minutes and propose what changes make sense for the next iteration. Take two minutes to silently collect your thoughts and then go around the room and quickly share.

Bonus Topic (Optional)

An optional question to consider asking the group is "If your money and your time were funding this pilot, would you invest in another month of development, or would you pivot?" This is a great way to gut-check the scores above and confirm that everyone is on the same page. It also provides the opportunity to frame value in a way that's more personal than if you are just spending the company's money.

Key Takeaways

Iteration is where your pilots shift from ideas to real outcomes, and it only works when your team is aligned, trusted, and committed to learning together. The most successful pilots rely on short learning loops where feedback is steady, honest, and directly shapes what you build next. You must evaluate the model, the prompts, the data, and the user experience with equal discipline because any one of them can accelerate progress or stall it. Failing fast should not be considered a failure; rather, it is a means of determining whether to refine, pivot, or scale. With this foundation in place, you are ready to move into the next stage and begin tracking the actual impact of your work.

CHAPTER 6

Track Impact

Do or do not. There is no try.

—Master Yoda
Star Wars: The Empire Strikes Back

Stop Trying. Start Proving.

Most teams move into this stage with a mix of excitement and uncertainty. You have something that works well enough to show people; the feedback you've received thus far is that it's useful, but you are not sure if it delivers enough business value to warrant an investment. You're trying to articulate the value, but you need more than anecdotes from your user feedback session. Track Impact works hand in hand with Iterate because every adjustment you make should be tied to a measurable signal, allowing you to close the loop. This is where you replace those "gut feels" with tangible evidence, allowing you to make decisions that leadership can stand behind.

In this chapter, we will first explore the typical business case patterns for technology investments. This will help establish the foundation for how you should approach tracking impact. Next, we'll talk about measuring business outcomes based on these patterns and your specific use case. Then we'll dive into different ways to collect feedback and measure the impact. Finally, we'll help roll all of this up into a pilot scorecard to help lead your project team and inform your executive stakeholders.

J. Matfess, *Your New Colleague is a Copilot*, Inside Copilot,
https://doi.org/10.1007/979-8-8688-2619-1_6

Why Track Impact Matters More Than Ever

Tracking impact is not just a final step in your AI journey; it is something that you should plan for and continue to monitor along the way. It becomes one of the primary signals that determines whether your organization sees AI as an experiment or a capability worth funding. Leaders are dealing with constant noise from vendors, analysts, and competitors, and they need a way to separate hype from value. When you track impact in a disciplined way, you give them the clarity they need to make confident decisions.

Impact tracking also builds trust with the groups relying on you to guide their adoption journey. It shows that you are not guessing and that you are willing to validate whether your solution truly addresses a meaningful business problem. This is important because most organizations do not have unlimited time or budget to chase ideas that feel promising but never deliver. In fact, many organizations are seeing their technology budgets decrease. When you provide repeatable evidence that your pilot is creating value, you are helping your leaders understand what deserves the next stage of investment, and perhaps what projects should be defunded or have their funding reallocated.

Organizational Goals

Before we start diving into business cases or what to measure, let's go ahead and take a step back and look at the bigger picture. What are some of your organization's objectives that your Senior Executives have been communicating either to Wall Street or to the enterprise as a whole? Perhaps your executive leaders are communicating a vision of being an AI-enabled organization, being customer-obsessed, or striving to be a trailblazer in your industry. You are going to want to understand the bigger picture of where your executives are trying to take your organization and begin not only mirroring some of their language but also evaluating whether what you're piloting might have a material impact on those goals.

This is an example where you might need to meet with different leaders within the organization or with individuals who represent their perspectives. The intent would be both to understand individual departmental goals and then see if any objectives span across multiple departments. The more entrenched your use case can be in solving numerous objectives, the higher likelihood you can expect to see it funded when it comes to scaling it beyond your pilot. Part of that analysis should not just include the organizational goals but also align them with the various business case patterns for technology investments we'll discuss next.

Business Case Patterns for Technology Investments

Organizations invest in technology for various reasons, and typically, part of the decision-making process involves establishing a business case. Since AI is still an emerging field, you should anticipate a healthy amount of scrutiny from your executive leaders as they review the business case behind your project. The makeup of these business cases will vary from organization to organization, but directionally, they tend to fall into the following three categories:

> **Return on Employee** - The organization is actively choosing to make an employee-centric investment. This could be for a variety of reasons, including but not limited to attracting and retaining top talent, demonstrating a commitment to career development, and staying competitive with competitors who may be equipping their employees with similar capabilities.

Return on Investment – This is a standard framework for evaluating any business investment. You have pre-investment costs, including time, head count, operating costs, and maintenance costs, among others. The intent is to understand the cost before investing and then capture the relevant metrics to understand the actual impact of the change on those criteria.

Return on the Future – This is very similar to the reason why you would invest in research and development efforts. You have a hypothesis that there is a future state business case that this technology can unearth, and you are investing in the future benefit that it may bring. Many pharmaceutical companies are evaluating AI to help bring future drugs to market faster.

Understanding the business case category is helpful because it will provide greater context for what you should be measuring. It also informs what your executive leaders will be looking for in terms of how you are tracking impact. It will also help provide initial direction on the business outcomes you can realistically measure. I have seen some project teams actually step through these three categories of business cases with their leadership as a show-and-tell exercise to ensure that everyone is on the same page about how they should be thinking about this pilot.

Defining Measurable Outcomes

The whole point of a pilot is to prove something, not to launch something for the sake of it. Measurable outcomes give you the ability to show progress that is grounded rather than intuition or enthusiasm. When you define these outcomes early, the team knows exactly what success looks like and what it does not. This clarity prevents scope creep, confusion, and the typical last-minute scramble to justify results that were never defined. Scope creep is a real problem in technology solutions, as there is always "one more thing" that can make a solution better. It's balancing the benefits vs. costs and impacts that will be necessary to help keep your project on the rails. Focusing on business outcomes is a helpful North Star for minimizing the impact of scope creep.

Well-defined business outcomes are specific, practical, and simple enough that anyone on your team could repeat them verbatim. You want to avoid abstract goals like "improve productivity" because they leave too much room for interpretation. Instead, choose metrics that directly tie to the user problem you are trying to solve, such as reduced time per task, fewer manual steps, or improved accuracy in a repeated workflow. These are the kinds of measurements that sponsors appreciate because they translate directly into impact.

As we discussed in Chapter 4, you will likely need to leverage a mix of quantitative and qualitative measures to articulate this impact. It is important, however, to acknowledge that not every outcome can or should be quantitative, especially in the early stages of AI adoption. Sometimes, the most valuable signals come from the tone of user feedback or the repeat usage patterns that show people trust the solution. These qualitative indicators often tell you more about long-term viability than a single chart or dashboard. When you combine them with the right quantitative measures, you get a complete picture of whether the pilot is working.

As you define your outcomes, keep in mind that they shape the rest of your iteration plan. They influence what data you gather, what feedback loops you design, and how you prioritize the next round of improvements. They give your team the confidence to celebrate progress or the courage to pivot when something is not delivering. Most importantly, they turn your pilot into evidence that leadership can stand behind without hesitation.

Performing A/B Testing

In specific scenarios, you may need to run A/B tests to gather the quantitative metrics needed for your use case. A/B testing, if you are unfamiliar, is a controlled way to compare two versions of something to see which one performs better. You present Version A to one group of users and Version B to another group. Then you measure to understand the differences between the two groups and determine whether the solution you are developing is having the intended impact.

An example might be testing an AI use case that helps summarize meeting minutes and provides a list of action items, owners, due dates, and other relevant information. You can test the efficacy of your solution by having one group of Project Managers complete this task as they normally would, without AI. You can measure how long it takes them to generate the email; you can have the recipients of that update provide you with feedback on the readability of the meeting cap. Then you can measure the same time and effort that it would take with your AI solution. The difference in time to complete the task will make up your quantitative measurement.

Then you can survey those same recipients about the quality of the messages. You can ask them to confirm they understood the AI-generated recaps. Note, you shouldn't tell the recipients which messages were created by the AI vs. the Project Managers to help avoid any unintended biases in their responses. Their assessment of the readability, clarity, and overall quality of the recaps will serve as your qualitative measure. Together, the quantitative and qualitative measures contribute to the overall impact measurement of your solution. The narrative you should be aiming to tell is that not only did AI help to reduce the time it takes to perform that recap, but also that the quality of the recap was hopefully more readable, as AI isn't overburdened with a multitude of tasks that are all due at the same time.

Quantitative Tracking

We have talked quite a bit about what to track against, but we haven't talked much about how to actually do it. Depending on your role in the organization, you might be focused on developing a common framework to roll up impact across the enterprise. Alternatively, you might just be focused on your project's use case. Regardless of role, developing a plan to measure the quantitative impact of your agent is an essential step for tracking the effects of your solution and confirming whether additional investments are warranted.

The first step you should take when considering measuring the quantitative impact of your solutions is to identify if there are any internal tracking capabilities available. You will want to check both the platform that you are using to build out your AI use cases, as well as any other ancillary analytics solutions in your organization's Enterprise IT portfolio. If there are no built-in analytics capabilities, you should ensure that, as part of your Sprint planning, you include user stories to capture activities and build out reporting capabilities. Remember, it's not enough to just track the activities; you will also want the ability to present them to your executive leadership team.

When I talk about built-in tracking capabilities, there are some AI platforms that will provide you with tooling to help facilitate the capture and reporting of your solution. For example, Copilot Studio, Microsoft's low-code agent development platform, includes a built-in savings calculator that you can use to start tracking savings. As you can see in Figure 6-1, Microsoft provides options to begin tracking savings per run of your agent or savings per "tool".

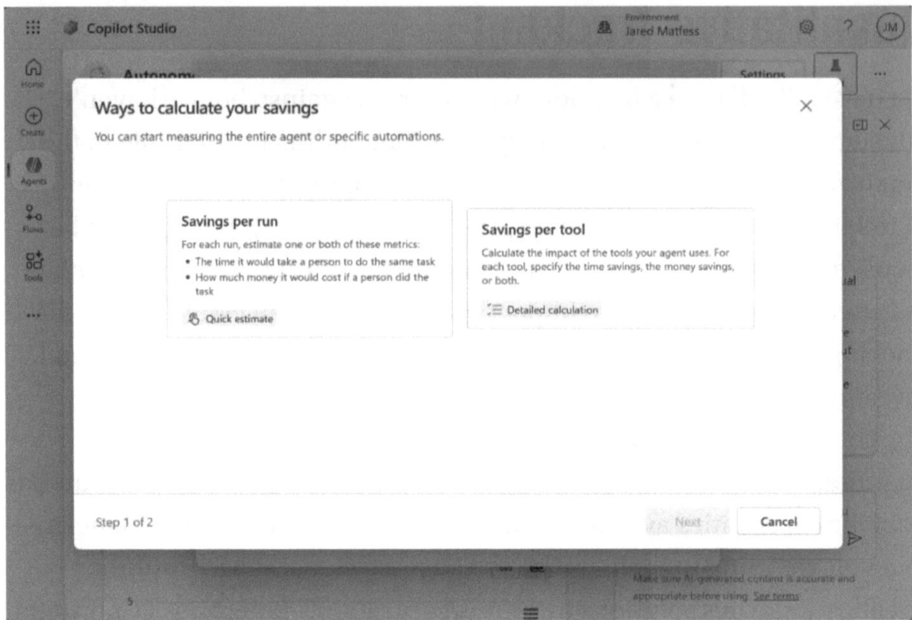

Figure 6-1. *Copilot Studio: Configure "Savings per run" or "Savings per tool"*

The "savings per run" is considered a "quick estimate," allowing you to quickly calculate the cost and effort if a human were to complete the same task. Alternatively, the savings per tool is a more detailed estimate based on the tools that the agent uses to perform tasks. Microsoft's definition of a tool is a configuration that performs a transaction in a third-party system. For example, an agent that connects to Salesforce to create a new opportunity is using the Salesforce "tool" to perform that transaction.

In the "Calculate savings per run" screen, you can then fill in the average time saved and money saved, as shown in Figure 6-2, to calculate your total savings per agent engagement.

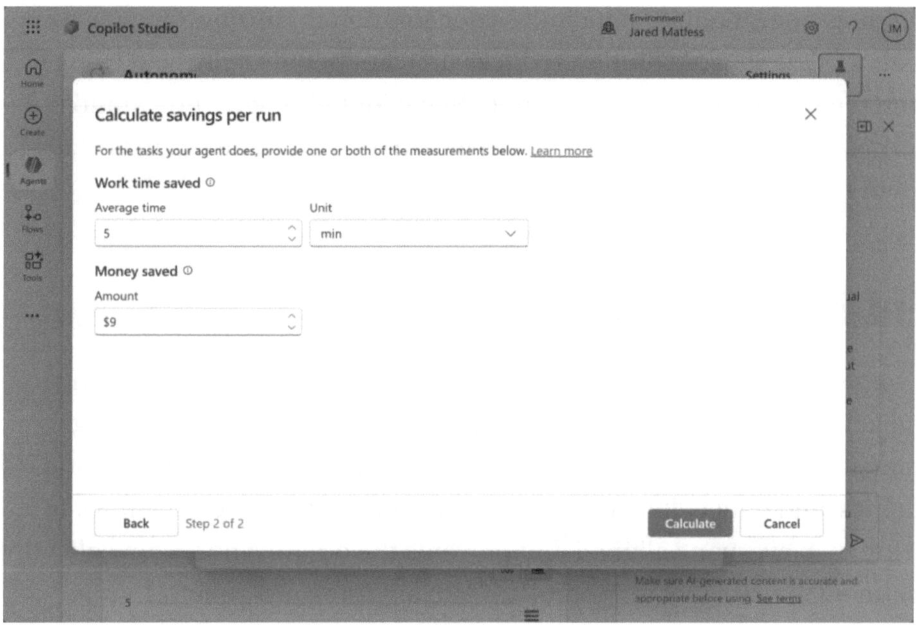

Figure 6-2. *Copilot Studio: Calculating "savings per run"*

The Role of User Behavior in Impact

One of the most underrated aspects of measuring AI impact is the behavioral change that emerges once users trust the solution. Trust tends to show up in small but meaningful patterns, such as people returning to the tool without being asked or recommending it to their peers. These patterns often appear before your hard quantitative metrics begin to shift. They are a leading indicator that your pilot is moving in the right direction. This is also something that you will want to pay close attention to when considering what the level of effort might be to scale your solution to a larger subset of the organization.

It is helpful to think of user behavior as part of your impact story. AI succeeds when it becomes part of someone's routine, not when it simply produces a technically correct answer. This evolution from piloting to building a new habit that includes your solution in the flow of work is huge. Without that, if your solution reduces time but people still avoid using it, then the value is not being captured. Behavior helps you understand not only whether the solution works but whether your organization is ready to adopt it at scale.

Enterprise Tracking

As organizations scale multiple AI pilots across departments, tracking impact becomes more complex. This is where an enterprise tracking framework becomes essential. A good framework defines the categories, metrics, and data collection practices that every team should follow. It helps keep everyone aligned and prevents the organization from collecting scattered metrics that do not roll up into anything meaningful.

An enterprise framework also gives executive leaders a clear view of their entire AI investment portfolio. They can see which pilots are creating the most value, which need attention, and which should be paused. This level of visibility helps them make smarter decisions about budgets, resources, and long-term strategy. Without a framework, every pilot becomes an isolated story, and leaders struggle to understand its broader impact.

Typically, you will want to either build or buy a solution that can serve as both the authoritative inventory of your AI solutions and a means of reporting impact. Beyond individual efforts and impact, you will probably also want to help articulate the overall AI activity within your organization. For example, AvePoint's AgentPulse solution, as pictured in Figure 6-3, shows you the usage of the agents.

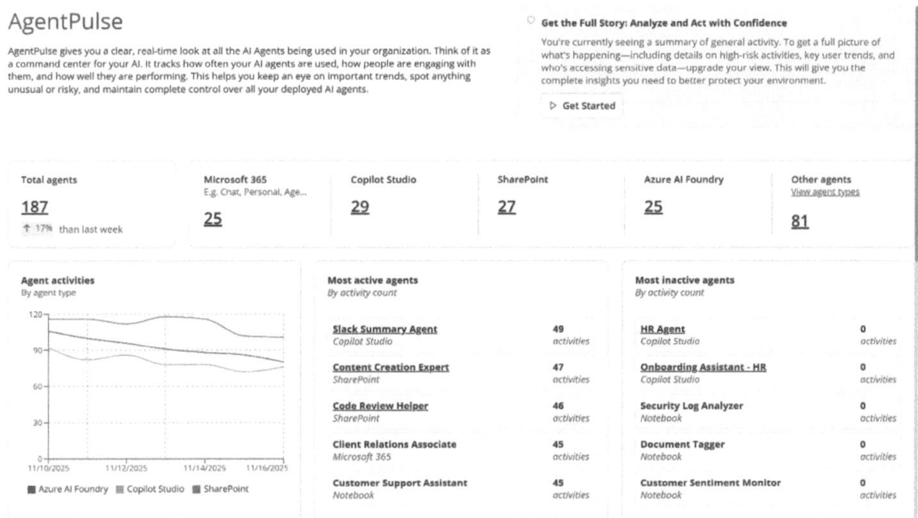

Figure 6-3. *Example: AvePoint's AgentPulse AI Agent Reporting Solution*

Additionally, they have extended their reporting beyond just the business impact being driven by the agents but also to what's happening in the overall AI ecosystem. Their AgentPulse reporting solution also highlights the individuals that are building AI agents and using them. They also have extended their reporting into the data being surfaced through agents as pictured in Figure 6-4. Their solution highlights agents that are accessing the most files, which is interesting from both a business impact and cybersecurity perspective. Agents are more commonly being viewed by Security professionals as a potential attack vector for data exfiltration. Also, their solution highlights file classification, so you can get a glance at potential data security risks.

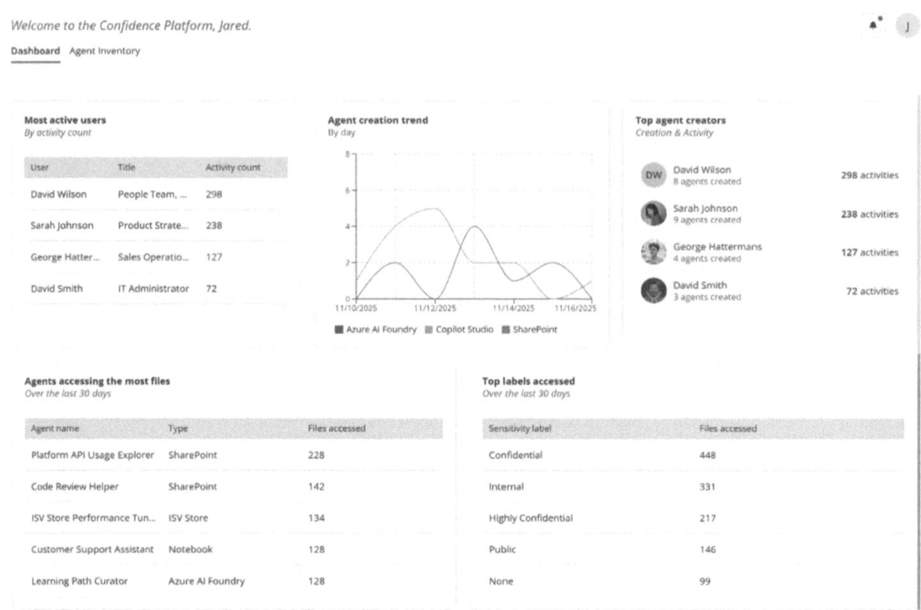

Figure 6-4. *Monitoring Users and Data*

Communicating Results

Once you have collected your quantitative and qualitative evidence, you need to package it so leadership can consume it quickly. Remember that, typically, executives do not want long reports filled with technical details. They want clarity about the impact, the decision you recommend, and what support you need next. A simple, well-structured presentation is more effective than an exhaustive data dump or technical details. Exceptions are, of course, expected if your senior stakeholders have a special interest in the technical details; however, from my experience, when the team is evenly split between business and technology stakeholders, you're better off keeping your report-outs at a high level.

Additionally, your communication should also focus on the story, not just the numbers. Explain why the pilot mattered, what changed, and what the organization should do next. It's helpful to also help connect the dots between this pilot and any broader organizational goals. Leaders respond well to confident recommendations grounded in evidence, and when surrounded with familiar language or initiatives that they may be trying to gain credit for. When your narrative is clean and supported by both qualitative and quantitative insights, it becomes far easier for them to approve scaling your solution.

Using Scorecards to Drive Repeatability

Scorecards give your organization a reusable structure for tracking results across multiple pilots. A scorecard is a simple way to track your pilot's performance against the outcomes you defined at the start. It organizes your metrics, baselines, and current results in one place so leaders can quickly see what is working and what still needs attention. A good scorecard creates clarity, consistency, and a repeatable model for future AI projects. They make it easier for teams to speak a common language, which helps leaders compare outcomes across departments.

Additionally, when done well, a scorecard keeps the team focused on the right things. It encourages transparency and removes the guesswork from deciding whether a pilot is performing as expected. It also becomes a living document that updates as your solution evolves and serves as a key storytelling tool for your executive leaders.

Scorecards are also useful for cross-functional alignment. When teams see impact framed consistently across the enterprise, they develop a shared understanding of what success looks like. This encourages consistency and quality as new teams begin their AI journey. It also helps prevent siloed decision-making by bringing everyone back to the same expectations. Lastly, since everyone's yearly goals and objectives are different, co-creating the pilot scorecard together is an exercise in helping to set up your project team for financial success. Ideally, they will help to contribute to the scorecard in a way that will provide their own reporting chain with both quantitative and qualitative measures that reflect their contribution.

BUILDING A PILOT SCORECARD

1. **Pilot Purpose**

   A short description of the business problem you are solving, and the outcome you expect to realize through the technical solution being developed.

2. **Success Metrics**

   List the signals you will measure. Keep them specific and tied to the goal.

   - Accuracy or quality target:
   - Adoption or usage target:
   - Time saved per task:
   - Cost avoidance or efficiency gain:
   - Risk reduction or compliance improvement:
   - User satisfaction target:

     (Optional: Define how each metric will be measured and by whom.)

3. **Baseline vs. Current Pilot Performance**

   Next, track your baseline against your observations through your pilot using Table 6-1. This will help to not only serve as a means to understand progress, but it will also serve as a key input for any further iterations of your solution.

Table 6-1. *Baseline vs. Current Pilot Performance*

Metric	Baseline	Current Pilot Performance	Notes
Accuracy			
Adoption			
Time Saved			
Cost Avoided			
Risk Reduced			
Satisfaction			

Key Takeaways

Tracking impact is about much more than collecting numbers. It requires you to tie your pilot to your organization's bigger goals, define clear outcomes, and measure both quantitative and qualitative signals intentionally. Some of the most valuable insights come from user behavior, because trust and habitual use often precede your charts' movement. When you focus on business outcomes, user patterns, and transparent evidence, you create a story that leaders can rely on to decide what should scale, what needs refinement, and what should be retired. As you move into Chapter 7, you will use these insights to establish governance and cultural practices that enable AI to grow responsibly across the entire organization.

CHAPTER 7

Embed Governance

Trust is built in drops, and lost in buckets.

—Kevin Plank
Founder of Under Armour

Why Governance Matters Now

By the time you reach this stage of IGNITE, your organization has seen the potential of AI in action. You have inspired people to care about what is possible, gauged your readiness, selected pilots that matter, iterated through the messiness, and tracked the impact in ways leadership can trust. Now comes the part that most organizations underestimate until it is too late. You need a governance foundation that can support AI as it moves from scattered experiments to a scaled capability.

Governance is often misunderstood as a brake pedal that slows innovation. Good governance acts more like lane markings with soft bumpers on either side. It gives people confidence to accelerate because they know where they can drive safely and where they cannot. When governance is designed well, it becomes an enabler rather than an obstacle that prevents you from moving forward. It helps leaders make decisions faster, reduces surprises, and creates a shared understanding of how AI should operate within the enterprise.

J. Matfess, *Your New Colleague is a Copilot*, Inside Copilot,
https://doi.org/10.1007/979-8-8688-2619-1_7

This chapter focuses on building that foundation. You will learn how to establish durable governance practices, shape organizational culture, define decision rights, set responsibility boundaries, and keep AI adoption aligned with business expectations. You will also learn how to prepare your entire organization for a future where AI is woven into every workflow instead of isolated inside a handful of teams or processes.

Embedding Governance into Your AI Operating Model

As mentioned, governance should never be a final checkpoint at the end of a project. If you treat governance as a destination, you will always be reacting to problems instead of preventing them. Instead, governance is most effective when embedded at every stage of the lifecycle. The goal is not more paperwork, more SharePoint sites to review, or more individuals to seek approval from, which would slow down your projects. The goal is predictable decision-making and safer, faster innovation that will ultimately help ensure you realize your desired business outcomes.

So, what is governance exactly? Governance is the structure that defines how your organization makes safe, consistent, and predictable decisions about technology, including AI. It sets the guardrails for how data is used, who is accountable, and how solutions move through their lifecycle. Practically, it's the combination of policies, procedures, and standards that are published within your organization that will guide project teams on how to implement a new capability successfully. At its core, governance creates confidence that AI can scale without introducing unnecessary risk or confusion.

An operating model describes how your organization works day to day, including the roles, processes, decision paths, and systems that keep everything moving. When you embed AI into the operating model, you make it part of the regular rhythm of work instead of a separate project or experiment. This reduces handoffs, eliminates rework, and prevents the "wild west" scenario that can creep in when people get excited about AI and start experimenting without guidance. And one of the most critical aspects of governance is the people that you include in co-creating the governance model that fits best for your organization, and those who help to inform others as a means to ensure it is integrated into how teams work.

Your Greatest Resistor: Your Culture

Governance rarely fails because of frameworks. It usually fails because your organization's culture refuses to adopt them. You cannot simply publish a policy and expect people to align their behavior with it. Culture shifts slowly, so you need to influence how people think about creating, using, and scaling technology.

When it comes to AI governance, your teams will need to adopt several new habits. They need to think more intentionally about data quality, lifecycle management, access controls, and responsible design. They also need to understand that risk is not always apparent at first glance. Poorly labeled data, a forgotten test file, or a misconfigured permission can derail an otherwise successful rollout. And despite all the excitement about the potential capabilities of this solution, you will likely find yourself stalled from making any further progress until these issues are resolved.

Leadership plays a major role in shaping this culture. When executives treat AI as a strategic capability instead of a novelty, it signals to the rest of the organization that governance is not optional. Teams follow the tone set from the top. When leaders consistently reinforce why guardrails matter, people internalize the message. Culture also grows through repetition. As teams build AI solutions, they will need to practice working within containers, validating permissions, capturing decisions, and documenting outcomes. Over time, these practices stop feeling like extra work and become how the organization operates.

Governance Step 1: The AI Working Team

Before you begin pulling together documents or decisions, you must first assemble the cross-functional team that will guide your organization through the chaos of AI. Your goal is to ensure representation from both the business and the technology sides of the house so that a single perspective does not shape decisions. This includes individuals who understand your data landscape, system architecture, operational processes, and frontline realities. When these voices come together early, you prevent blind spots and help the organization move forward with confidence.

The early working team should also include someone from Legal, Privacy, or Risk, even if they are not full-time contributors. Their presence helps the group understand boundaries before the project accelerates into areas that could create long-term exposure. They can highlight regulatory considerations, help interpret policy obligations, and provide early guidance on what might require formal review. Most importantly, their involvement builds trust with leadership because it shows you are thinking about safety and responsibility from day one.

This group is not meant to become a permanent committee with endless meetings. Instead, think of it as the initial steering function that sets direction, establishes early guardrails, and provides clarity for the teams that will build and scale AI solutions. They establish the first version of your governance model, identify key responsibilities, and help outline the processes that will support future growth. Once the foundation is set, the team can evolve, expand, or hand off duties to more specialized governance bodies as your AI maturity increases. However, one of the first tasks that this AI Working Team will need to complete, which can be used to shape your policies, procedures, and standards, is an intake process, which we'll talk about next.

Governance Step 2: The Intake Process

Once you have your AI Working Team established, the next step is to create a predictable and straightforward intake process for new AI ideas. This process becomes the front door for every request, whether it is a small experiment, a new agent, or a high-visibility automation sponsored by a business leader. The intent is not to slow people down, but to ensure that all work follows the same path so the organization can evaluate ideas consistently. It shows that you are already working toward becoming an AI-enabled organization and are receptive to change.

A good intake process usually starts with a short set of questions that will help the working team understand the purpose, expected impact, data needs, and risks associated with each proposal. You are not trying to collect a novel's worth of detail or ensure that they have every potential risk mapped out. You are trying to gather enough information to determine whether the idea is viable, whether the data is appropriate, and whether the request should move forward. This initial screening protects downstream teams from surprises and allows the organization to prioritize work based on business value and readiness rather than enthusiasm alone.

The intake process also helps shape your policies, procedures, and standards by highlighting common patterns. Over time, you will begin to notice themes in the types of requests you receive, the data sources people want to use, and the risks that repeatedly surface. These patterns give you insight into where guidance is lacking and which guardrails need strengthening. When the intake process becomes routine, teams know exactly where to go, what information to provide, and how to engage with the governance model, which makes AI adoption feel organized rather than overwhelming.

When crafting your questions, you should consider what might help you determine if this use case even warrants the need for AI. With the major hyper-scalers such as Microsoft, Google, and even AWS pushing for all organizations to adopt AI quickly, there is a need to calm that chaos with a reality check. Not every business problem requires an AI-enabled solution. In fact, the solution can often be achieved with existing workflow-based technology or even robotics process automation (RPA), rather than overcomplicating it with AI. Speaking of, let's work through a quick exercise to develop a few questions that will help you with making that determination.

AI OR NOT AI?

This exercise helps you distinguish between what requires AI and what can be solved through existing technology. It also guides you through defining the right questions for your organization's intake process.

Step 1: Review the Use Cases

Review the list below and decide whether each scenario truly requires AI or if it could be solved using rules, workflow automation, or traditional software. The goal is to help you sharpen your instinct for which requests should enter the AI intake process and which should be routed elsewhere.

1. A manager wants automatic reminders sent to employees who have incomplete training.
2. A customer service team wants an agent who can summarize long case files and propose next steps.
3. A department wants a tool that sends forms to a shared inbox and organizes them into folders.
4. A project team wants an agent that can review inconsistent product descriptions and propose standardized versions.
5. A regional office wants to track expenses and notify people when they exceed thresholds.

Step 2: Evaluate the Scenarios

Evaluate the previous scenarios with the following questions to help navigate whether the use case is best solved with AI or through other technologies.

1. Which scenarios involve prediction, interpretation, or reasoning?
2. Which ones rely on structured rules or predictable outcomes?
3. Which ones require understanding unstructured data such as documents, conversations, or images?

Step 3: Review Answers

1. **Automatic reminders for incomplete training**

   This scenario does not require AI. It is a rules-based workflow with predictable triggers and outcomes. A simple automation or scheduling tool can handle this more reliably and with less overhead than an AI solution.

2. **An agent that summarizes long case files and proposes next steps**

   This is a strong AI use case. It requires interpreting unstructured data, summarizing key points, and applying reasoning to suggest a path forward. An AI agent built in Copilot Studio or another LLM-powered environment is appropriate.

3. **A tool that organizes forms emailed to a shared inbox**

   This is not an AI requirement in most cases. A combination of workflow automation, inbox rules, or a low-code solution can classify and route structured forms with little complexity. AI may only be needed if the forms are extremely inconsistent or contain unstructured free text that must be interpreted.

4. **An agent that reviews inconsistent product descriptions and proposes standardized versions**

   This is well-suited for AI. It involves pattern recognition, rewriting, and aligning content to a standard, which requires natural language understanding. This is the type of work where generative AI adds real value.

5. **Tracking expenses and notifying people when thresholds are exceeded**

   This is a rules-driven scenario that is better handled with automation or built-in finance system alerts. Unless the request includes unstructured data analysis, forecasting, or anomaly detection, AI is unnecessary here.

Step 4: Create Your Intake Questions

1. **What business problem are you trying to solve?**

   Why it matters– Most requests jump immediately to a desired tool or feature. This question forces the requester to describe the actual problem, which helps the working team determine whether AI is even necessary and whether the problem is meaningful enough to pursue.

2. **What does success look like for this use case, and how will you measure it?**

   Why it matters – Clear outcomes are essential for evaluating impact. If the requester cannot articulate what success looks like, the team will struggle to assess whether the solution is worth building or whether expectations are realistic.

3. **Who is the primary user, and what workflow does this support?**

   Why it matters – Governance depends on understanding who will rely on the solution and how it fits into their daily work. This helps identify adoption risks, training needs, and potential operational impact.

4. **What data does this use case require, and where does that data currently live?**

   Why it matters – Almost every AI project fails or succeeds based on data readiness. This question helps surface where data quality issues, oversharing, missing permissions, or lifecycle gaps might create risk or delay the project.

5. **Does this use case involve regulated, confidential, or sensitive information?**

   Why it matters – Legal, risk, and privacy teams need early visibility into scenarios involving protected data. It prevents surprises later and ensures the working team applies the right container or risk tier from the start.

6. **Why is AI required for this scenario instead of workflow automation or existing tools?**

   Why it matters – This question helps filter out non-AI requests. Many problems are better solved with rules-based automation, built-in platform capabilities, or simple integrations. This prevents AI from becoming a hammer looking for nails.

7. **How frequently does this task occur, and how much time does it take today?**

   Why it matters – Frequency and effort help determine business value. A task that happens once a quarter may not justify an AI build. A task that happens 200 times a week absolutely might.

8. **What systems or applications does this use case touch?**

   Why it matters – Governance bodies must understand the operational and architectural blast radius. Some systems have strict controls, limited connectors, or change management requirements that must be planned for.

9. **Who will own this solution after it is deployed?**

   Why it matters – Ownership is often the biggest governance gap. If no one owns the solution, no one maintains it, monitors it, or ensures that it continues to operate safely. This question prevents orphaned agents.

10. **What risks or unintended outcomes concern you about this use case?**

    Why it matters – Requesters often know their domain-specific risks better than anyone else. This question surfaces potential pitfalls that the working team might not otherwise anticipate, such as misinterpreted context or decisions that could affect customers.

By working through these questions, you create the clarity needed to evaluate new AI requests with consistency instead of guesswork. You also give your governance team the information they need to prioritize work, spot risks early, and route ideas to the right place. Over time, this simple intake process becomes one of the most reliable ways to keep your AI portfolio organized and focused on the outcomes that matter.

Governance Step 2: Establishing Responsibility Boundaries

One of the biggest sources of tension with AI adoption is the lack of clarity about who owns what. IT expects business teams to handle specific responsibilities. Business teams expect IT to take care of them. Security teams assume controls are in place. Makers assume guardrails already exist. Meanwhile, no one has a shared understanding of their role.

To embed governance, you need to define responsibility boundaries that align with how your organization works. These boundaries typically fall into five categories:

1. **Data Ownership** - Who decides what data can be used for AI workloads and under what conditions?
2. **Solution Ownership** - Who governs the lifecycle of the AI solution once it is deployed?
3. **Risk Ownership** - Who is accountable if something goes wrong, and how decisions are documented.
4. **Operational Ownership** - Who maintains the environment, updates models, and monitors usage signals.
5. **Adoption Ownership** - Who drives training, change management, and long-term engagement.

You do not need perfect definitions on day one. You need something actionable that teams can follow while you refine the model through lived experience. What matters is that ownership is visible and agreed upon. When people know what they are responsible for, governance stops feeling ambiguous and instead becomes part of everyday work.

Governance Step 3: Who's the Decision-Maker?

Organizations for decades have grappled with identifying owners, responsibilities, and in many circumstances, decision-making. Similar to a project RACI (responsible, accountable, consulted, informed) chart, your company will need a similar structure for AI. AI solutions introduce new types of decisions that many organizations have never had to consider. Teams need to know who approves access to sensitive data. They need clarity about what qualifies as "safe enough" to deploy. They need rules about when experimentation can proceed and when it must pause.

Clear decision rights allow teams to move with confidence. They remove the friction caused by inconsistent approvals, confusion about who must sign off, or delays caused by unclear escalation paths. When decision rights are not defined, teams move either too slowly or too recklessly. Neither scenario serves the business.

You can think of decision rights as a set of traffic lights for your AI ecosystem:

- **Green** – Proceed without formal approval because guardrails already cover the risk.
- **Yellow** – Proceed with caution and notify specific stakeholders.
- **Red** – Stop until governance partners have reviewed and approved the activity.

The value is not in the colors themselves. It is in the shared understanding they create when your organization starts to accelerate piloting new capabilities, and is looking for repeatable decision-making processes to ensure that they move forward while also minimizing risk.

Step 3: Digging into the Data

Let's take a quick pivot from people and policies to the elements that will help further refine your approach: the data. One of the first places that enterprises dive into AI is with one of the many popular GenAI-as-a-service offerings. Some examples of these include Microsoft 365 Copilot, Google Gemini, ChatGPT Enterprise, etc. What they quickly realize is that these tools lean heavily on the data you've already got, especially that big, messy pile of unstructured content sitting around in your environment.

And that's where the challenge comes in. Unstructured data often isn't curated. Ownership is fuzzy, and over time, people don't exactly put in the love and care to keep it clean and well-labeled. So, when you start experimenting with these AI tools, you might find yourself in a situation where you're surfacing content that really shouldn't be surfaced. It's easy to accidentally overshare, giving broader access to files and data that not everyone should have. And that means you're amplifying existing security and governance issues that were kind of hidden before AI came into the picture.

In other words, these new AI capabilities sort of force your hand. They highlight the need to step up your game on data governance and take action to keep things in check.

Starting Remediation: Prioritizing the Most Sensitive Data First

The next piece of the puzzle is figuring out how to actually start fixing the problem. Step one is all about understanding where your issues are and then deciding what to tackle first. Every organization has some sensitive data. Healthcare providers have their Personally Identifiable Information ("PII") and Personal Health Information ("PHI"); finance has Financial Industry Regulatory Authority ("FINRA") and Payment Card Industry ("PCI") concerns; aerospace and defense contractors have International

Traffic in Arms Regulations ("ITAR") and export control data. The point is, it's not about whether you have sensitive data; everyone does. It's about identifying where sensitive data is overexposed in your environment.

Once you know that, you can prioritize what to remediate first. The reality is you're never going to make unstructured data perfect, and that's okay. It's about layering on multiple lines of defense, remediating what you can, educating your users, and accepting that a certain level of risk is just part of the deal. AI is just one example. Every technology brings a bit of risk, and the goal is to find a balance between locking things down and still moving forward.

Tooling and Inventory: Navigating the Gaps in Reporting

Once you get into the nuts and bolts of discovery, there's a reality check around the tools you're using. Not every reporting capability is going to give you the whole picture, especially when we're talking about unstructured data in a big, complex tenant. A lot of the out-of-the-box tools from your service providers might only cover a subset of your environment.

Take, for instance, some of the data access governance reports that Microsoft provides as part of their SharePoint Advanced Management capability, as shown in Figure 7-1. When you dig into the fine print, you'll notice a specific line: *"Activity reports help you track potential oversharing activities that occurred in the last 28 days."*

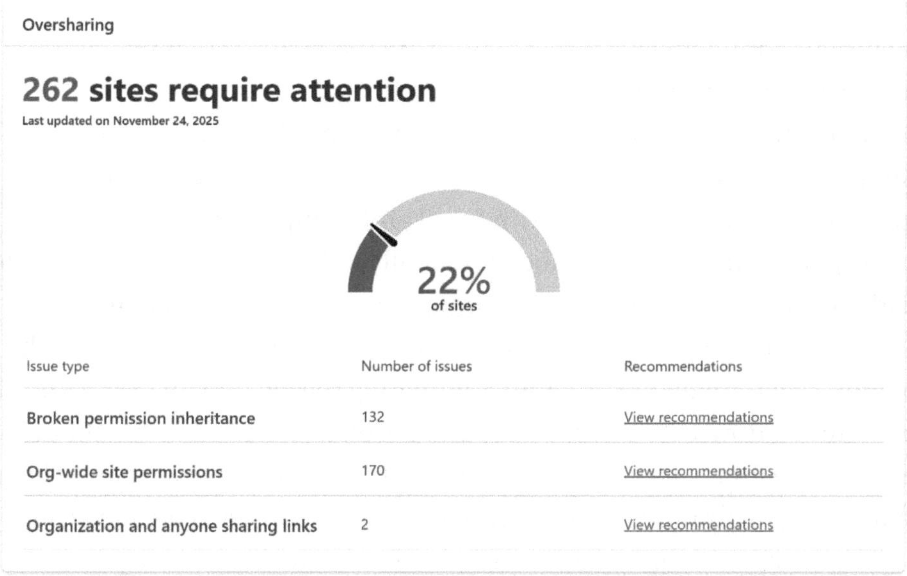

Oversharing

262 sites require attention

Last updated on November 24, 2025

22%
of sites

Issue type	Number of issues	Recommendations
Broken permission inheritance	132	View recommendations
Org-wide site permissions	170	View recommendations
Organization and anyone sharing links	2	View recommendations

Figure 7-1. *SharePoint Advanced Management Activity Reporting*

This means the report is only returning results for which there were activities during 28 days. That means any stale or dormant data isn't even on the radar from a risk perspective, and you're not really seeing the actual current state of oversharing and overexposure in your tenant. In other words, the native reports might give you a starting point, but they're probably not the end-all solution. You might need to look at building or buying something more comprehensive to get a real sense of where your risks lie and to figure out a proper remediation plan.

Remediation: It's More Than Just Labels!

So, let's talk about the reality of remediation. It's not just about slapping a label on a file and calling it a day. Sure, data classification is a valuable concept, and you'll hear the hyper-scalers and third-party vendors talk about it as a key step for AI readiness. But labeling is not really the heart of the issue. The real question is: does the file have value? Is it relevant? Are the permissions actually correct? Those are the nuances that matter more than just a classification tag.

In practice, I've seen many organizations start down the path of classification only to realize it's a massive, multi-year project. You end up having to define standards with Legal and Compliance, onboard pilot groups, drive adoption, and label potentially millions of files. And if you do math, that can push out your AI adoption timeline by years, not months.

So, the bottom line is that while classification might be one tool in the toolbox, real remediation is about automating the cleanup of overexposed data, cutting down the ROT: redundant, obsolete, trivial data. It's about making sure that what you keep is actually helpful and safe to share. That's what's going to improve the quality of your AI responses in the long run.

When embedding AI governance, focus on three data principles:

1. **Right Data** - Ensure the data being used is accurate, curated, and aligned with the use case.
2. **Right Access** - Validate that only the people who should have access do.
3. **Right Lifecycle** - Keep your data governed over time, not just during the pilot stage.

This is where you may look to mix both native capabilities like Microsoft Purview and third-party tools like AvePoint's Confidence Platform, as pictured in Figure 7-2, to help with not only performing a one-time remediation but also ensuring that going forward, you have governance guardrails in place to help maintain data and security hygiene.

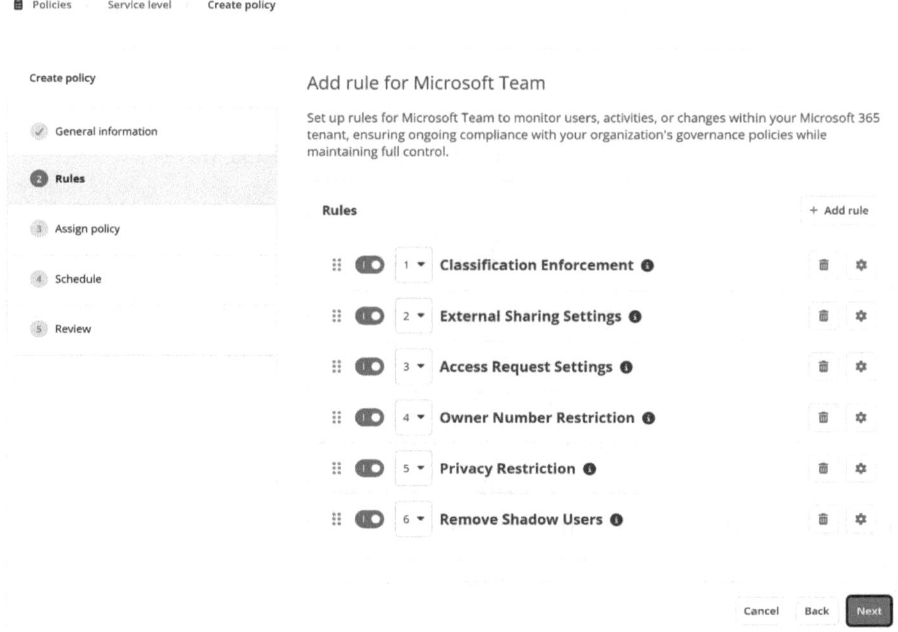

Figure 7-2. *AI Confidence Policies to Govern Microsoft Teams*

Building Guardrails Instead of Gates

Governance should never be a gate that blocks progress. The entire purpose of governance is to create a safe environment where people can innovate responsibly. If teams feel like governance slows them down, they will find workarounds. Workarounds lead to shadow AI, which introduces risk, fragmentation, and inconsistent results.

Guardrails do something different. They allow people to build without constantly asking for permission. They establish clear, reasonable, and easy-to-follow expectations. When guardrails are visible, makers feel empowered instead of restricted. Examples of guardrails that work well include

- Standard templates for documenting prompts, assumptions, and risks
- Automated checks for permissions, sensitivity labels, and lifecycle management to help reduce ROT data
- Tiered environments with clear expectations for experimentation versus deployment

Guardrails scale in ways manual approvals never will. They also reduce dependency on a small group of experts, which becomes important as more teams begin working with AI. And the guardrails that work the best are the ones that include your business users, like a site recertification process, as shown in Figure 7-3. Empowering your business owners unlocks a shared accountability model where IT owns the platform, and the business is responsible for managing its data.

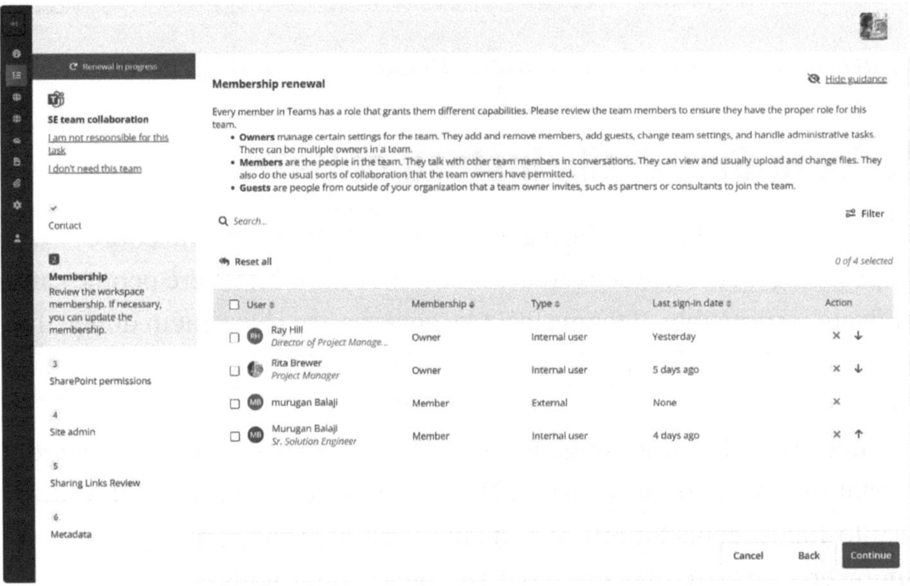

***Figure 7-3.** Workspace Lifecycle Management*

Avoiding AI Sprawl

One of the most prominent risks organizations face in AI adoption is solution sprawl. This happens for many reasons, including individuals who just want to experiment with this emerging capability, multiple teams building similar agents, and, primarily, a lack of governance. Without any overarching governance processes, duplication becomes common, adoption becomes fragmented, and admin teams struggle to keep track of what exists.

To prevent agent sprawl, you need to create a central catalog of solutions. The catalog does not need to be complicated. It simply needs to track ownership, purpose, risk level, and lifecycle state. When teams can see what already exists, they are less likely to build duplicates. This not only reduces sprawl but also helps rein in solution-related costs. There may be existing solutions, such as Microsoft's Agent 365, as shown in Figure 7-4, that can help inventory agents across your various cloud providers.

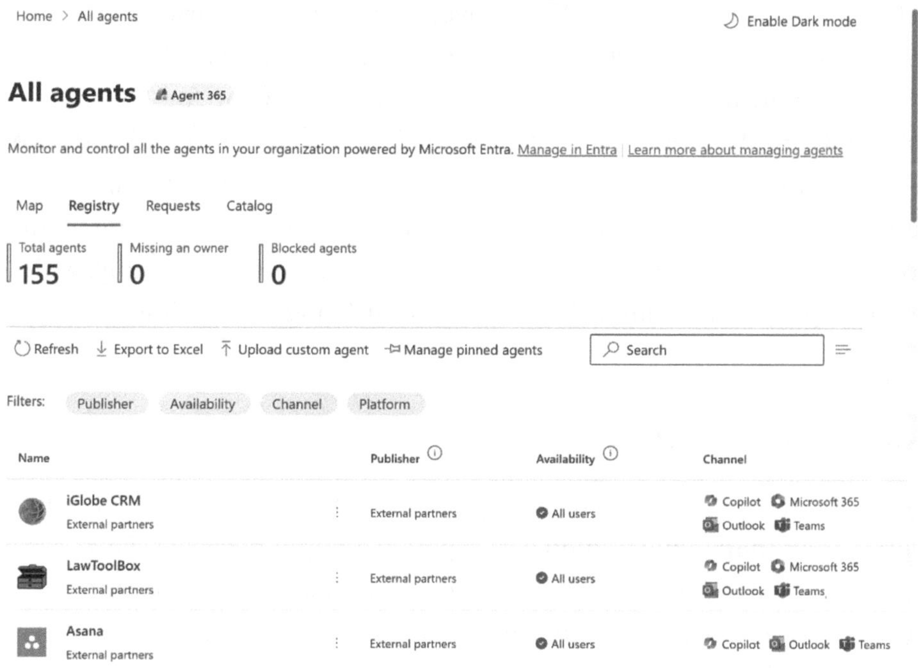

Figure 7-4. *Microsoft's Agent 365 Inventory Platform*

Tying It All Together by Embedding Governance in Your Operating Model

Tying everything together requires a shift in mindset. Governance cannot sit on a separate island while AI moves forward in pockets of the business. If governance is absent from the day-to-day operating model, teams will treat it as optional. That is when mistakes creep in, solutions get built in isolation, and decisions get made without the proper context or oversight. The goal is to make governance feel less like a compliance task and more like a natural part of building and scaling AI.

To do this well, you need to bring governance into the same rooms where your teams plan, design, test, and release their work. It should be shown during sprint planning when teams decide what to build. It should show up in design reviews when people talk through data sources and access needs. It should show up in product demos when teams evaluate risk alongside functionality. When governance is visible during these moments, it becomes part of the rhythm and not a separate chore.

Most importantly, embedding governance sets you up for sustainability. AI adoption is not a single project with a start and end date. It is a capability that needs to grow with your teams, your systems, and your business strategy. By bringing governance into your operating model now, you create the environment where AI can expand responsibly, with fewer surprises, and with a clearer path toward long-term value.

Key Takeaways

AI governance works when it is designed to support how people already work, rather than being treated as a separate compliance layer. This chapter reinforced that governance succeeds when it is transparent, predictable, and embedded in everyday decisions. When teams understand the purpose behind the guardrails, know who owns what, and follow a consistent intake process, they move faster with fewer surprises. Strong data practices also proved essential. AI amplifies whatever you feed it, so cleaning up oversharing, improving data quality, and establishing ownership become non-negotiable steps for safe scale.

The other important learning is that culture is the deciding factor. Policies and frameworks provide structure, but people bring it to life. Leadership must reinforce that governance is a business enabler, not a barrier, and teams must see it in action during planning, design, testing, and deployment. When governance is visible in the operating model and supported by a shared understanding of roles, responsibilities, and decision paths, the organization shifts from experimentation to sustainable AI maturity. That is how governance strengthens culture and culture strengthens governance, creating an environment where AI can grow responsibly over time. And now that you have the foundation in place, the next step is preparing your people with the AI literacy and training needed to use that foundation with confidence.

CHAPTER 8

Building AI Literacy

Technology is nothing. What is important is that you have faith in people, that they're basically good and smart, and if you give them tools, they will do wonderful things with them.

—Steve Jobs
Co-founder and Former CEO of Apple

Preparing Your People for an AI-First Workplace

I still remember my first office job after years of working retail at the upgrades counter at our local CompUSA store. It was a shock to the system going from a world where I was on my feet, dealing with customers or sorting stock rooms, to suddenly being in an environment where everyone had a computer at their desk. Work came in via email, decisions were made in conference rooms, and the whole rhythm of "doing" shifted to coordinating and organizing. As a 20-something, that shift really made me rethink what "work" meant. It was about building new habits and relearning what productivity looked like.

Now, in this chapter, we are going to unpack a similar shift, but for AI literacy. We are on the edge of change, where it is no longer just humans doing all the tasks. Instead, we are learning how to offload specific tasks to software that can act in very human-like ways. We must help people

J. Matfess, *Your New Colleague is a Copilot*, Inside Copilot,
https://doi.org/10.1007/979-8-8688-2619-1_8

understand where the guardrails are, what AI should and shouldn't do, and how to set the right expectations for different people in your organization. That's what we're tackling here: making AI literacy approachable and practical for everyone involved in this transformation.

AI Literacy for Leaders

Let's start right at the top: one of the biggest hurdles in any AI transformation is setting the right expectations with your leadership. We've discussed economics and the business cases for tech investments in earlier chapters. Still, here it's really about helping your C-suite and senior leaders get what AI actually is. There's often a misconception that we're at a point where AI can outright replace roles—that we can stop hiring people or that entry-level jobs will vanish. We're nowhere near that point. AI is more like a powerful productivity tool, think Wi-Fi, VPN, or the cloud. It changes how we work, it shifts roles a bit, but it absolutely doesn't eliminate the need for people. In fact, people are the ones who make AI worthwhile.

So, a strong recommendation is to start with your leadership. You should give them a targeted training initiative that helps them understand what AI can and can't do. That way, they can champion its potential without stirring up unnecessary fear or churn. In the end, that's going to help everyone adopt the technology more smoothly, because they'll understand it's here to enhance their work, not replace them.

BUILDING YOUR LEADERSHIP AI LITERACY CURRICULUM

In this exercise, we will create a high-impact AI literacy curriculum that respects the limited time your leaders actually have. The goal is to meet each executive where they are by understanding their baseline knowledge before you teach anything new. This helps you focus on what matters most to them, rather than giving a generic overview that misses the mark. Ultimately, you want a curriculum that equips leaders to guide the organization confidently through AI adoption.

Step 1: Run a Quick Pre-training Survey

Before finalizing the curriculum, send a short survey to your executives. Ask them about their current understanding of AI, what they're most curious about, and any specific concerns they have. It's not a test; it's just to gauge their starting point so you can meet them where they are from a learning perspective.

Step 2: Identify Core Topics Based on Survey Results (5 Minutes)

Now that you have a sense of where each executive stands, choose the core topics that matter most to them. Maybe your CIO gets a deep dive on integration, while your CEO focuses on strategic impact.

Step 3: Break It into Role-Specific Micro-Sessions (5 Minutes)

Divide those topics into 15-minute micro-sessions that reflect each leader's priorities. For one leader, that might mean a myth-busting intro, and for another, a case study relevant to their part of the business.

Step 4: Include One Relevant Hands-On Example (5 Minutes)

Pick a demo or interactive example that ties directly to what each executive cares about. It could be a quick look at an AI tool in their specific area of focus, or something more generic that you will be rolling across the enterprise, like Google Gemini or Microsoft 365 Copilot.

Step 5: Wrap Up with a Personalized Resource List (5 Minutes)

Finally, give each leader a resource list that matches their interests, so they can explore further if they choose.

This exercise gives you a simple structure for building leadership confidence without overwhelming their schedules. It helps you anchor the conversation in what matters most to them while avoiding unnecessary detail that slows momentum. Most importantly, it sets the tone for the rest of your AI literacy efforts by showing that training can be focused, practical, and respectful of everyone's time.

Teaching the Rest of the Organization

As we step into this section, let's build directly on what we covered in the "Gauge Readiness" chapter of the IGNITE framework. When you gauge readiness, you're not just diagnosing where your organization stands; you are also gathering insights that will shape your AI literacy plan. In other words, the readiness assessment is your compass. It tells you which parts of the organization are already open to AI and which might need a more thoughtful, careful introduction to address any concerns.

When building an AI literacy program for your enterprise, be prepared for unique training needs across the organization. At the same time, many like to point to the rapid adoption of ChatGPT as proof that consumer-grade AI technology is easily picked up. You must temper that with the fact that hundreds of millions of people have never used ChatGPT and will be skeptical of AI as a help rather than a replacement for their roles. My wife is a nurse and has just started using ChatGPT, despite the fact that she has observed me using it almost daily to do everything from product research to ensuring that an email I draft doesn't come across as snarky.

So, in this section, we're taking that readiness map and using it to tailor our approach to AI literacy across the rest of the organization. Some teams will need just a light touch, while others will need more in-depth support.

And yes, personas are part of the story, but the real key is letting that readiness gauge guide how you meet each group's unique needs.

Understanding the Key Persona Groups

Once your personas are clear, the next step is shaping literacy paths that make sense for each of them. This is where your Gauge Readiness insights come back into the picture. That chapter helped you understand where the organization is strong, where it is vulnerable, and where different groups stand in terms of confidence, capability, and data hygiene. Now you translate those insights into learning experiences that meet people at the right level.

Start by identifying which groups scored high on readiness. These teams are primed for faster adoption. They may already have strong digital habits, sound data practices, or leaders who encourage experimentation. Given their literacy path, they should have space to experiment. These teams learn quickly when they can open a tool, try something simple, and immediately see what changes. They do not need long lectures or heavy conceptual overviews. Instead, they would benefit from practical examples, demonstrations, and a space to apply what they've learned.

Next, look at the middle-scoring groups. These teams may be open to AI but lack consistency in data practices, have uneven comfort levels, or work in processes that move slowly. Their literacy path should focus on clarity and confidence-building. They need to understand what AI is for, how it helps, and how to use it responsibly without feeling overwhelmed. Scenario-based walkthroughs and guided practice work well here to help move from theoretical to practical. Additionally, they may need extra "human intervention" via AI coaching, to help reinforce their learning and to help give them confidence that they're able to be successful despite perhaps not being highly technical.

Finally, address the groups that scored low on readiness. These teams are not behind. They simply need more intentional support. Their literacy path should start with a foundational understanding, clear examples of how AI supports their role, and reassurance about what AI will not do. This group benefits from structured introductions and thoughtful pacing. The goal is not to rush them. The goal is to help them feel safe and supported as they learn.

Designing these literacy paths is less about creating different programs for every team and more about adjusting the intensity, depth, and pacing of your content. You are matching the learning experience to the group's starting point. When you do that well, adoption becomes smoother, fear decreases, and everyone can build confidence step by step.

Teaching the Rest of the Organization

Once you understand your personas and design literacy paths that match their readiness levels, the next challenge is delivering the training in scalable ways. Most organizations make the mistake of thinking AI literacy requires a massive program, a long curriculum, or full-day workshops that no one has time to attend. In reality, the most effective literacy programs are those that fit naturally into how people already work. You do not need to flood people with training. What works best are small moments that help people build confidence one step at a time.

The first place to start is with short, focused learning moments. These can be 10-minute videos, 15-minute demos, or quick scenario walkthroughs that show how AI can help with a task people already perform. Short content respects everyone's time and lowers the barrier to learning. It also makes it easier for teams to absorb information in small pieces without feeling pulled away from their day-to-day responsibilities.

Next, you want to introduce hands-on opportunities. People learn AI best by trying it, not by watching someone else use it. This can be as simple as a guided exercise during a team meeting or a short practice prompt people try on their own. The key is giving them a chance to feel the technology in action. When people see a task get easier, faster, or clearer because of AI, their confidence begins to grow.

You should also consider group-based formats that encourage shared learning. Not every team needs a formal workshop, but many benefit from collaborative sessions where they can ask questions, share wins, and talk through where AI fits into their workflow. These can include short office hours, weekly "ask me anything" sessions, or informal drop-ins with a subject-matter expert. Group learning builds community and reinforces that they are not navigating this change alone.

Finally, make sure your literacy efforts are supported with ongoing, lightweight documentation. This does not need to be a full training portal. It can be a simple library of examples, practice prompts, common questions, and short guides tailored to the persona groups you identified earlier. When people have a small, searchable resource they can return to, they gain a sense of stability and consistency. They know where to go when they have a question or want to try something new.

Delivering AI literacy at scale is about meeting people where they are, providing formats that fit their work rhythm, and creating simple ways for them to build capability over time. When you do this well, the training becomes less of a program and more of an ongoing support system that helps the entire organization move forward with confidence.

BUILDING YOUR AI LITERACY PROGRAM

In this exercise, we will create a simple, scalable plan for delivering AI literacy across your organization. This exercise helps you map the right delivery formats to the right persona groups so you are not guessing how to reach people. The goal is to design learning experiences that fit naturally into daily work rather than forcing people into long, disruptive training sessions.

Step 1: Select Three Persona Groups to Focus On

Look at the persona groups you identified earlier and choose three that represent the broadest range of needs. For example, you might pick frontline staff, knowledge workers, and managers. Write down their current readiness level and any known challenges each group faces with AI adoption. If possible, a good prerequisite to this step is sending out a survey to potential persona groups to benchmark their current knowledge and readiness.

Step 2: Match a Primary Learning Format to Each Group

For each persona, assign a primary training format that you believe will best help reach them. For example:

- Short video or micro-lesson(s)
- Guided hands-on practice
- Live office hours or drop-in sessions
- Team meeting demos
- Simple job aids or quick reference sheets

Choose the format that aligns best with their readiness and workload, and then begin to brainstorm some of the specifics that might further bring AI to life for them.

Step 3: Add One Hands-On Touchpoint for Each Persona

Decide how each group will get a chance to try AI directly. This can be a short exercise, a practice prompt, or a simple workflow example. The goal is to give them a meaningful experience without creating extra steps. Write down one hands-on activity for each persona. An example might be creating a basic inventory lookup agent that a frontline worker could use to check stock, rather than having to type it on their mobile device.

Step 4: Identify Supporting Resources

List one or two lightweight resources you can provide to each persona group. This might include a small FAQ, quick start tips, a cheat sheet of prompts, or a list of recommended use cases. These resources should be short and easy to reference.

Step 5: Confirm the Cadence

Decide how often you will deliver training touch points for each group. Some teams may benefit from a weekly ten-minute demo. Others might only need a monthly office hours session. Select a cadence that supports learning without overwhelming schedules but also keeps them engaged as you continue to scale AI within your organization.

How to Sustain AI Literacy Over Time

Launching AI literacy is only the beginning of your journey. The real value lies in nurturing that understanding as technology evolves and people start using it in more complex ways. AI tools change quickly, and so do the expectations people have for how they fit into daily work. Sustaining literacy is about creating an environment where people feel supported long after the initial training wave is complete.

One of the easiest ways to keep literacy alive is by setting a regular refresh cadence. This does not need to be a formal training cycle. It can be a simple quarterly touchpoint where you introduce new capabilities, address emerging questions, or share examples of what teams across the organization are doing. Short, predictable updates help people stay informed and build confidence over time. The objective is to ensure that people in your organization can see progress.

Another important strategy is to identify internal AI champions. Every organization has people who enjoy learning new tools and helping others and are natural connectors. When you empower these individuals as "AI shepherds," you create a distributed support network that keeps momentum going. These champions model responsible use, surface common questions, and help you understand where extra training may be needed.

Additionally, you should consider enabling them through a digital community that supports them in working together to share best practices, lessons learned, and impactful success stories. Using a virtual community, like what is shown in Figure 8-1, will provide a safe space for experimentation, sharing, and growing. It will also help drive greater adoption as you'll connect experts and evangelists across the organization to surface top use cases and pinpoint areas of your business that may require additional support. Finally, having a community will also drive adoption, as it ensures that the individuals you have nominated as your evangelists are learning and growing from their peers.

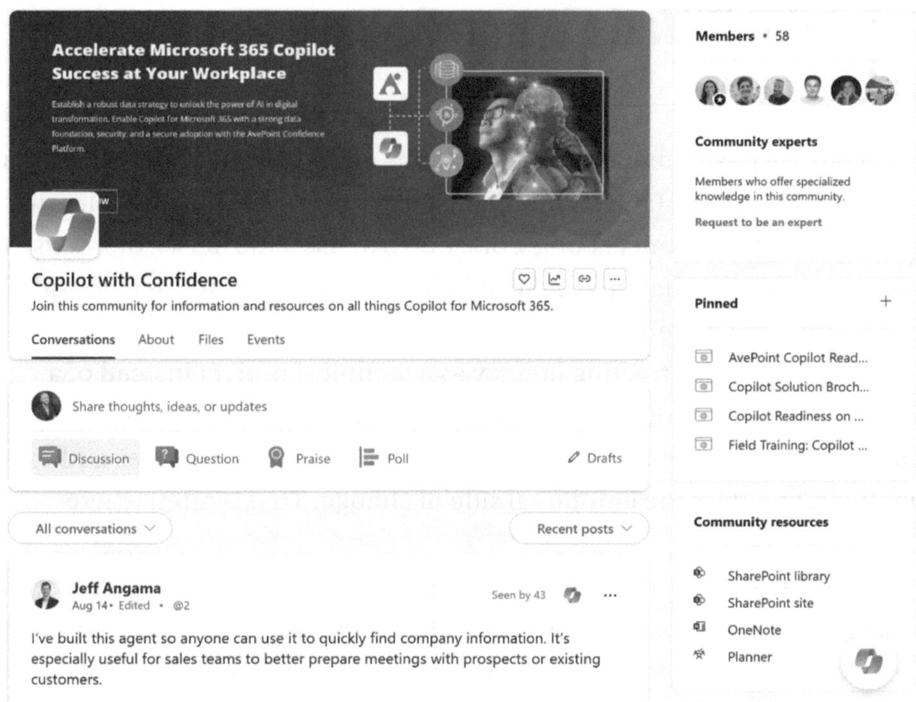

***Figure 8-1.** Example of an Internal Champions Network*

Note The example community site shown in Figure 8-1 uses Microsoft Viva Engage. You may need to confirm with your IT team whether Viva Engage is available for your organization.

Finally, sustaining literacy requires keeping the learning practical. As AI becomes more integrated into workflows, your training must stay grounded in real tasks, not abstract concepts. When people see immediate value in their day-to-day work, literacy becomes a habit instead of a one-time event. The goal is steady growth, not perfection, and your role is to give people the consistent support that allows them to build that confidence step by step.

Common Pitfalls When Rolling Out AI Literacy

Even with the best intentions, organizations often stumble when they try to introduce AI literacy. One common mistake is overwhelming people with too much content at once. Long workshops, dense slide decks, or intensive programs can create fatigue and confusion. People need space to absorb information, not a firehose.

Another pitfall is treating literacy as a technical project instead of a people project. AI adoption is far more about behavior, habits, and trust than it is about the tools themselves. If you focus only on features and functions, you miss the emotional side of change. That is often where resistance takes root.

Organizations also run into trouble when they skip over groups that seem skeptical or slow to adopt new technology. These teams are not barriers. They are opportunities. When you support them with patience, clarity, and practical examples, they often become strong advocates.

A final pitfall is assuming one training path fits everyone. Personas exist for a reason. Each group needs something different, and literacy efforts fall apart when leaders try to compress everything into a single, generic program. Tailoring your approach builds trust and helps people feel seen, which is exactly what you want during a transformation of this size.

SPOTTING THE COMMON PITFALLS

In this exercise, we will work to help you identify where your organization may be slipping into common AI literacy pitfalls so you can correct them early. We will focus on reflecting honestly on your rollout efforts and make minor adjustments before they turn into bigger barriers.

Step 1: Review the Four Pitfalls

Write down the four pitfalls from the previous section: overwhelming content, treating literacy as a technical project, ignoring skeptical groups, and using a one-size-fits-all approach.

Step 2: Score Each Pitfall

For each pitfall, give your organization a simple score from 1 to 5.

- 1 means "Not happening here."
- 5 means "This is definitely happening."

Keep the scoring quick and honest.

Step 3: Identify One Adjustment

Look at the pitfalls that scored highest. Choose one and write down a small adjustment you can make within the next two weeks. It should be realistic and actionable. For example, shortening a training deck, scheduling a Q&A session for a skeptical group, or tailoring content for a specific persona.

Step 4: Share with a Partner

If you are completing this exercise with a team, share your scores and any adjustments with one other team member. The goal is to create visibility and make pitfall avoidance a shared effort.

By the end of this exercise, you will have a quick snapshot of where you may be slipping into common traps and a simple plan to correct course before those issues slow your AI literacy efforts.

Measuring Progress and Confidence

As you roll out AI literacy, you need a way to understand whether it is working. Measuring progress is not about testing people or scoring their knowledge. It is about observing whether confidence, comfort, and capability are growing in the right ways. The signs are usually subtle at first.

You might notice that people are using AI tools more often or asking more targeted questions about how to apply the technology to their work.

One of the simplest ways to measure progress is through sentiment. Short pulse surveys can give you a quick read on how people feel about AI after training sessions or hands-on practice. You can also track which teams are requesting more examples, guidance, or office hours. Increased curiosity is a strong indicator of rising confidence.

You can also look at usage patterns. Are people experimenting? Are they trying prompts? Are they applying AI in small but meaningful ways in their workflow? These signals show that literacy is turning into action. You do not need perfection. You need momentum, and usage data helps you see where it is growing within your organization. And not only do you need to see this data, but you also need to be able to present it back to leadership. Data visualization can be a great storyteller, as shown in Figure 8-2, where you can show adoption week over week, as well as the patterns of usage. This specific example is using AvePoint's tyGraph Copilot Analytics reporting. There are a number of first- and third-party AI reporting solutions to help you measure adoption.

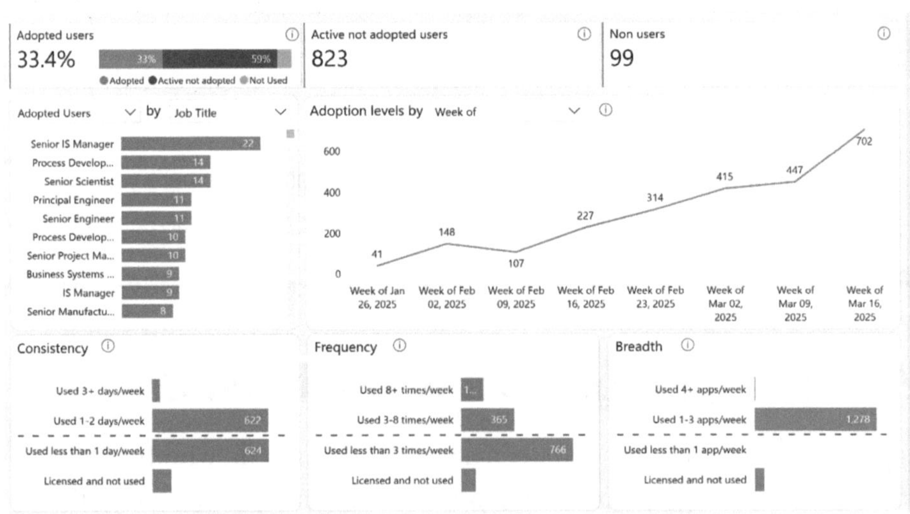

***Figure 8-2.** Example of Data Visualization for Adoption Tracking*

Finally, measure progress by listening. People will tell you what they need if you create a safe space for questions and feedback. When they begin to ask more profound questions about accuracy, quality, or workflow integration, it shows that they are shifting from a basic understanding to practical problem-solving. That is the real mark of a successful literacy program. It means your training is not just landing, it is sticking, and your organization is becoming more confident step by step.

Teaching People to Think with AI

AI literacy is not only about learning new tools or technologies. It is also about learning a new way of thinking and then building the habits to sustain adoption over time. Most people approach AI as if it works like a traditional search engine or a clever shortcut. They ask a quick question, hope the output is correct, and feel discouraged when the result falls short. Thinking with AI requires a different mindset. It is a skill that builds over time, and it is one of the most valuable things you can teach your organization during this stage of the transformation.

The first part of this shift is learning to ask better questions. AI works best when you give it structure and clarity. When people learn to define the goal, describe the desired outcome, or break a big problem into smaller pieces, the quality of the output improves immediately. This is not about writing fancy prompts. It is about slowing down long enough to think through what you need. Once people understand this, they stop expecting AI to read their mind and start guiding it with intention.

The second part is learning to evaluate the output. AI can sound polished even when it is wrong. One of my favorite examples is when I asked Microsoft's Copilot in Excel what kind of charts it can create. It confidently told me it could generate pie charts, scatter plots, bar charts, etc. As soon as I asked it to make a pie chart, it told me it was unable to create charts but here are the steps needed to build a pie chart. It is important to teach people to review the output, challenge it, ask follow-up questions, and this is helpful to ensure that your users avoid placing blind trust in a system that still needs their oversight.

The third part is understanding when to use AI and when not to. Some tasks are perfect for AI because they are repetitive, structured, or require large amounts of information. Other tasks depend on human experience, empathy, or situational awareness. Also, within AI, there are times when it may make sense to have it generate content vs. times when it may be better to have it spot your biases. For instance, when I'm writing an email to senior leaders, I always write first and then ask AI to review. However, when I'm working on a blog post, I have no issue with AI generating a first draft that I can further refine. Helping people recognize the differences among use cases will help prevent misuse and, hopefully, avoid harmful AI outcomes. It also reinforces the learning idea that AI is a partner, not a replacement, and to have it work with you vs. for you.

Teaching people to think with AI changes how they approach their work. Instead of seeing AI as a threat or a shortcut, they begin to see it as a powerful tool that sharpens their thinking and expands their capabilities. That mindset is what makes AI literacy sustainable. It helps the entire organization move forward with clarity, confidence, and a shared understanding of how to use AI responsibly and effectively.

Measuring Progress and Confidence

To make this chapter even more actionable, it helps to see how all the pieces fit into a simple 90-day plan. You do not need a large team or a massive budget. You need clear steps and a consistent rhythm. Here's a starting point for you to refine based on your own journey.

Days 1–30: Leadership Alignment and Awareness

Start with your leadership training snapshot. Run the survey, tailor the content, and give your executives a shared understanding of what AI can and cannot do. At the same time, begin raising awareness across the organization with simple communications and small examples of how AI supports everyday work. Your objective is to inform them of your company's investment, give them an introduction to the technology's potential use cases, and hopefully get them bought in to further support.

Days 31–60: Persona Mapping and Learning Path Design

Use your Gauge Readiness insights to define your persona groups and design learning paths for each one. Decide which formats work best for each group and prepare the micro-sessions, reference materials, and hands-on activities you will need.

Days 61–90: Delivery, Practice, and Confidence Checks

Begin rolling out your first wave of literacy programming. Keep everything small and focused, and record if possible so that you can solicit both human and AI feedback on how you perform. Host short demos, provide an opportunity for hands-on practice, and conduct one or two office hours sessions to help drive engagement. Close the loop with your confidence checks, including pulse surveys and longer self-assessments. Look for signals that the training is landing, and use that feedback to adjust your next cycle.

By the end of the first 90 days, your organization should have a clear sense of direction, a foundation of shared understanding, and the first signs of growing confidence. You will not be done, but you will have momentum, and that is far more important than perfection.

Key Takeaways

AI literacy is not a technical exercise. It is a people-centered effort that requires understanding, patience, and clear expectations. When you meet people where they are, they move forward with more confidence and less fear. When you tailor your approach to different persona groups, you respect the diversity of work styles and responsibilities across your organization. Your readiness assessment is the tool that guides everything. It tells you where to focus, how fast to move, and what kind of support people will need along the way.

Sustained literacy comes from small, consistent touchpoints rather than one-time training events. And as confidence grows, so does the organization's ability to adopt AI responsibly and at scale. Most importantly, AI literacy is the bridge between early experimentation and long-term transformation. It lays the foundation for our next chapter, where we'll take a lot of the theory we have outlined so far and integrate it into your organization as the new AI Operating Model.

CHAPTER 9

Designing Your AI Operating Model

The system is the product.

—Adam Richardson
Design Strategist and Author of *Innovation X*

AI Will Not Scale Itself

Early in my career, I worked on mergers and acquisitions from the IT side. My job wasn't just assessing systems, platforms, and application portfolios. It was also evaluating the people behind them. That often meant identifying duplication, finding new landing spots for retained IT staff within our primary outsourcer's organization, or facing the difficult reality that there might not be a new role for someone. It was one of the hardest responsibilities I ever had, and it taught me early on that so much of business success comes down to the operating model. How do groups come together to solve problems? What is the runbook for how work gets done? Where does accountability sit, and how do you know when something is finished?

J. Matfess, *Your New Colleague is a Copilot*, Inside Copilot,
https://doi.org/10.1007/979-8-8688-2619-1_9

I have been through many transformations in my career: from paper to electronic, from on-prem to cloud, and from desktop to mobile. AI is another transformation, but the pattern is familiar. Technology itself evolves quickly, but the real challenge is always the people. How do they learn? How do they adapt to changes in both the workplace and at home? From my experience, AI does not fail because the model is imperfect. It fails because the organization has not built the structure that helps people adopt it with confidence.

In this chapter, we will focus on how to create that future-state AI operating model. We will walk through the steps to clarify roles, processes, decision points, and handoffs. We will explore practical strategies that help teams adopt AI in a structured, predictable way without slowing down innovation. And we will highlight the common pitfalls that cause AI efforts to stall so you can avoid them. By the end of this chapter, you will have a blueprint for how your organization can run AI at scale, not as scattered experiments, but as a coordinated system that supports how people actually work.

What Is an AI Operating Model?

When I think about an operating model, I think about how work actually gets done. It is the people, the processes, and the technology, all working together in a predictable rhythm so the organization can deliver on what it promises. Some parts are written down and formal, while others are unwritten rules that teams pick up over time. At a basic level, it covers everything from the moment someone says they need something to the assignment of work to the completion and follow-up to make sure the job was done well.

But with AI, those traditional pillars need more structure. You cannot simply drop AI into the old operating model and hope for the best. You need clear ownership and accountability, so everyone knows who is responsible for decisions, outcomes, and guardrails. You need well-defined roles that cover sponsorship, oversight, execution, and feedback, because AI work pulls in people from different parts of the business in a way traditional projects never did.

You also need lifecycle processes that make sense for modern AI work. That includes how ideas come in, how they get evaluated, how the work is assigned, how quality is checked, what gets monitored, and what success even looks like. Without a defined workflow, AI efforts will scatter across teams, leading to inconsistent results. As someone that grew up in manufacturing, I have found my learnings from optimizing the flow of work through the shop floor to be similar to that of addressing operating models. The intent is to try and look for areas of friction in your processes, including what will cause delays or rework, and find opportunities to remove those impediments. In manufacturing, time is money; therefore, adopting that same manufacturing mindset will also be helpful when considering how you structure your AI operating mode.

Support and enablement matter just as much as the processes. AI adoption moves quickly, and people need a place to bring questions, escalate issues, and get help when something is unclear. Training, change management, and straightforward guidance all play a much bigger role than most organizations expect.

And finally, there are the tools and platforms. This is not just the AI model itself. It is the entire environment that supports it—the clouds, the systems, the governance layers, and all the places where the work gets built and monitored. Microsoft, AWS, and Google each bring different capabilities to the table, and your operating model has to account for how those ecosystems will support your people and your processes.

So, when you step back, the operating model is really the blueprint for how your organization will make AI real. It is the structure that keeps the work organized, the people supported, and the technology aligned. And if you get it right, it becomes the foundation that lets you scale instead of stall. Now that we have a clear picture of what an AI operating model is, we can break it down into the five pillars that make it work in practice.

Pillar 1: Ownership and Accountability

When you think about ownership in an AI operating model, it starts with clarity. Someone has to stand up and say, "This solution matters, and I'm responsible for making sure it delivers value." That person is the owner. They are not a symbolic figurehead. They are the one who understands the business problem, knows the stakeholders, feels the pain of the current process, and has a vision for how AI will improve it. In many ways, they are the product owner for the AI initiative. They set the direction, define success, prioritize features, and help make real-world decisions that keep the solution grounded in the right business outcome.

Ownership also includes understanding the boundaries. The owner does not need to know how transformer models work or how data pipelines integrate behind the scenes. But they must know what they are trying to achieve, who the solution impacts, and what "good" looks like in practice. They need to have enough familiarity with the work to provide steady guidance, approve key decisions, and explain the purpose to their team. Without this anchor, projects lose momentum quickly. You end up with a builder trying to guess what the business wants, which is a recipe for rework and frustration.

Now, accountability sits right beside ownership. It is the mechanism that ensures no AI solution drifts into a gray zone of abandonment. Accountability means that if a project starts to stall, or if the business owner becomes disengaged, someone can step in and say, "We need to stop, regroup, or reassign leadership before this goes any further." In a mature operating model, this usually falls to IT leadership, the AI governance group, or a steering committee. They are not there to micromanage. They are there to protect the organization from half-built agents, misaligned solutions, or tools that end up unsupported six months after launch.

Accountability also extends to quality, safety, and responsible use. If the owner is responsible for the vision, and the builders are responsible for creating the solution, accountability ensures that the work meets standards. It means someone is consistently checking alignment with business goals, making sure the data is appropriate, reviewing risks, and validating that the solution behaves the way it should. This is not about policing people. It is about creating predictable outcomes. Without this structure, AI solutions can quickly become inconsistent, confusing, or even risky.

Finally, ownership and accountability together set the tone for everything else in the operating model. They determine who makes decisions, who verifies quality, who speaks to leadership, and who communicates with consumers of the solution. When these two pillars are strong, the rest of the operating model becomes easier to build. When they are weak, the entire structure wobbles. AI cannot scale on enthusiasm alone. It scales on clarity—and that clarity starts with knowing who owns what and who ensures the work is delivered with integrity.

Pillar 2: Roles and Responsibilities

In the realm of AI transformation, defining roles and responsibilities goes far beyond just having a single owner. It's about creating a whole ecosystem of players who each bring a piece of the puzzle. When you move from a pilot phase into full-scale AI adoption, the landscape of roles shifts significantly.

At the heart of this landscape lies data ownership. This is a shared responsibility between business and IT. Business data owners curate and manage the content that AI relies on, while IT owns the platforms that house that data. It's a partnership: IT ensures the infrastructure is solid, secure, and scalable, while business owners ensure the data is accurate, relevant, and up to date.

But it doesn't stop there. You also need roles focused on learning and development. These are the people designing the training curriculum that builds AI literacy across your organization. They're the ones ensuring that everyone from entry-level staff to senior leadership understands how AI will change their roles and what new skills they'll need.

Then there are the builders themselves. This includes not just your traditional developers writing full-code solutions but also the business analysts and citizen developers using low-code platforms. They're responsible not only for building the AI solutions but also for ensuring these solutions align with responsible AI practices. They need to be aware of biases, incorporate human oversight, and educate the rest of the organization on the why, not just the how.

Finally, don't forget the legal and compliance roles. These folks are the bridge to auditors, regulators, and anyone who needs assurance that your AI practices are above board. They make sure that your operating model includes the right checkpoints and that you're always in a defensible position if someone asks, "Why did this AI make that decision?"

In short, Pillar 2 is about mapping out all these roles, understanding the responsibilities each one carries, and ensuring they all work together seamlessly. It's about aligning the right people to the right tasks, identifying gaps early, and communicating those needs up the chain so that your entire organization is set up for AI success.

IDENTIFYING ROLE GAPS IN YOUR AI OPERATING MODEL

This exercise will help you identify which key roles are already defined in your organization and which ones may still be missing. Use Table 9-1 to check off whether each role exists and note any specific gaps or considerations.

Table 9-1. *Organizational Roles*

Data Owner	Description	Exists (Y/N)	Notes
Executive Sponsor	Senior leader who champions AI adoption and unblocks resources and decisions.		
Business Product Owner(s)	Owns the business outcome, defines success, and prioritizes the road map		
AI Program Manager	Coordinates work across teams, manages timelines, and drives alignment		
Data Owner	Manages business data, ensures accuracy and relevance		
Data Steward	Handles operational data quality, metadata, and labeling		
AI Developer	Builds and implements AI features (full-code or low-code)		
IT Platform Owner	Owns hosting platforms and integrations for AI solutions		
Quality Leader	Tests accuracy, validates performance, and ensures responsible use		
Security Architect	Assesses security risks, reviews access patterns, and validates data boundaries		
AI Governance Lead	Oversees reviews, guardrails, intake processes, and lifecycle governance		
Support Desk Manager	Provides frontline and tier-two support for AI tools and agents		
Risk Management Lead	Evaluates operational, reputational, and business risks tied to AI use		
Change Management Lead	Manages communication, readiness, and adoption activity		

Pillar 3: Processes and Lifecycle Management

When we talk about the lifecycle of an AI solution, it all begins with intake. That's when someone in the organization identifies a business problem that might be solved with a technical solution, and AI seems like a candidate. That idea could come from IT, from the business side, or from anyone who spots an opportunity. Ideally, there should be a form or request that the person can fill out to help document the use case, the area of the business that would benefit from this new capability, and any other relevant information to help inform those reviewing the request.

Once you have that intake, the next step is evaluation. Someone or some group will need to assess whether AI is truly the right tool for the job. Not every problem needs to be solved with AI; sometimes a structured workflow or an existing tool is a better fit. This step is about making sure you're not reinventing the wheel when there's a simpler option available. It also means looking across the portfolio and being aware of whether other groups are solving the same or similar challenges. Again, the goal isn't to gatekeep or prevent innovation, but rather to ensure that funds are invested wisely and that groups can leverage each other's synergies where possible.

One of my favorite stories comes from an Executive Vice President of a large Financial Services organization. He was talking about how one of his teams was presenting a business case to replace an existing process with a Robotic Process Automation ("RPA") solution. The current process today involves a small group of individuals offshore performing the work. When he asked for the breakdown of IT costs vs. current costs, he noticed that the cost to run the systems and software that automate the process was almost three times what they were currently paying the offshore firm to do the work. Therefore, in addition to ensuring the use case is a fit, ensuring there is a positive ROI is rather essential when evaluating a potential use case.

After evaluation comes assignment, and at this point, especially early on in updating your operating model, you will need a project manager or similar role to shepherd the idea through planning and execution. That means working with your procurement team to ensure you have the appropriate budget in place to support any technical needs, or to bring in outside help to bring the idea to life. It also means organizing the necessary project management activities, such as creating a timeline, assembling the team, building a backlog, and establishing an appropriate meeting cadence to drive the effort forward. It also involves identifying the data owners and ensuring that security and risk management are part of the conversation from the start.

From there, you move into the actual development and agile processes. In addition to building or configuring your solution, you will need to start testing to confirm not only functionality but also accuracy and to ensure that the data sources being leveraged are appropriate for the audience. Eventually, once you have satisfied both the functional and technical requirements, your solution will be moved to a Production environment so your users can gain true hands-on experience. But lifecycle management doesn't end when the solution goes live. You need ongoing monitoring for adoption, compliance, and quality, making sure you're seeing the business value you expected and that there are no unexpected hiccups.

Finally, there's the long-term view. As your AI solutions evolve, someone needs to manage the portfolio, deciding when a more standardized solution might replace a custom-built tool and ensuring that older solutions are retired gracefully. It's all about keeping the lifecycle healthy from start to finish. You should be evaluating from both a cost optimization and a user experience lens to ensure that you are getting the most value out of your investment and that your solution is in the right ecosystem to support the current and future needs of your users. Mapping out this process is a key step in ensuring you have thought through the flow from idea to post-implementation, and a really great way to do so is to develop a service design blueprint for your new AI operating model.

Pillar 4: Support and Enablement

When it comes to Support and Enablement, it's crucial to think about these elements from the very start. Unlike traditional applications, AI systems often require a different kind of support approach. For instance, your helpdesk teams will need to understand that AI is intent-based and that nuances in language and prompting can significantly impact performance. This means that support resources, such as runbooks, need to be adapted to address AI-specific challenges.

Additionally, it's crucial to equip frontline support staff with proper AI training. They should be well-versed not only in the AI application itself but also in how it differs from traditional tools. This can involve hands-on training, sample applications, and scenarios that help them build proficiency in AI troubleshooting. You want to help them avoid a situation where they feel uncomfortable providing support to your users.

Moreover, self-service resources are key. Creating an intranet hub with FAQs, best practices, and community forums allows users to find answers independently and encourages peer-to-peer support. Often, peers can provide insights that are more contextually relevant than those offered by the IT team. In summary, support and enablement for AI are about preparing everyone involved and ensuring they have the tools and knowledge to navigate AI's unique challenges effectively.

Pillar 5: Tools and Platforms

A strong operating model is never just about the people and processes; it also depends on the platforms you choose to build on and how well you understand what those platforms are capable of. For most organizations, the core ecosystem will center around Microsoft, Google, Amazon Web Services, and OpenAI. Each of these companies ships updates at a pace that is hard to keep up with unless you make it someone's responsibility.

Your operating model should include a recurring practice of reviewing public road maps, joining private previews when appropriate, and maintaining relationships with your account teams to anticipate what is coming rather than react to it.

Part of this pillar is helping your organization make smart decisions about where to build. Sometimes a full-code solution is the right choice when you need deep control or custom integrations. Other times, a low-code or no-code approach is faster, cheaper, and easier to maintain. The goal is not to enforce one path. The goal is to build a muscle around evaluating trade-offs so teams can choose the right tool for the problem. When this thinking becomes part of your regular planning process, you avoid the drift that leads to inconsistent experiences and duplicate investments.

It is also worth recognizing that AI platforms behave differently from traditional enterprise tools. They evolve quickly. Features appear, shift, or retire in ways that can impact your support model, training plan, and architectural decisions. This makes platform awareness a shared responsibility among IT, security, data, and the makers closest to the work. When these groups stay aligned on where the platforms are going, it becomes easier to build responsibly and scale without surprises.

Finally, your tools and platforms should reinforce the direction of your operating model, not fight against it. When you understand how Microsoft, Google, and OpenAI shape their ecosystems, you gain the clarity to design for flexibility, longevity, and the future you know is coming.

VISUALIZING YOUR AI OPERATING MODEL

In this exercise, we are going to create a clear, end-to-end view of how an AI request flows through your organization, who owns each step, and where accountability sits. This blueprint becomes one of the most valuable artifacts in your AI operating model because it shows precisely how the work moves, who touches it, and how decisions are made.

Step 1: Map the Stages of the Service

Start by listing the primary stages that an AI request goes through in your organization. Aim for high-level stages first, such as

- Intake
- Triage
- Build or configuration
- Testing and validation
- Approval
- Deployment
- Monitoring and feedback

Do not overthink this. You are just creating an initial sketch, and this can and should be refined and updated when you have more data or examples.

Step 2: Identify the Actors

For each stage, write down the people or roles involved. This might include

- Business sponsor
- Product owner
- Maker or developer
- IT
- Security
- Data owner
- End users
- Governance reviewers

Try to stick to roles, not individuals, so the blueprint scales to more than just a couple of individuals.

Step 3: Assign Ownership

Now take a pass through the entire flow and mark who owns each stage. Ownership should be clear, singular, and reflect a team, not an individual. If you have more than one owner for a stage, you do not have an owner.

You can use a simple O/S/C notation:

- **O** = Owner
- **S** = Supporter
- **C** = Consulted

This helps keep accountability honest and ensures that your process will scale beyond just a small pilot.

Step 4: Capture the Touchpoints

For each stage, jot down the key interactions between teams. Think about

- Handoffs
- Approvals
- Decisions
- Required inputs
- Documentation
- Communication paths

These touchpoints are often where work gets stuck, so write them faithfully.

Step 5: Surface the Pain Points

After the flow and roles are mapped, ask

- Where are the bottlenecks?
- Where do requests bounce between teams?

- Where is ownership unclear or duplicated?
- Where is accountability missing?

Circle or highlight these areas. These become the top opportunities for improvement.

Step 6: Add Success Metrics

For each stage, list a small number of success signals. Examples include

- Intake response time
- Time to initial working solution
- Accuracy scores
- Test cycle time
- Approval cycle duration
- Feedback response rate

These metrics ensure the blueprint not only describes work but also helps improve it.

Step 7: Review the Blueprint with Your Teams

Share the blueprint with the people who do the work. Ask them

- What did we miss?
- Where is reality more complicated?
- Where are we making assumptions?

Your goal is not perfection. Your goal is alignment.

Final Outcome

By the end of this exercise, you will have a visible, end-to-end service blueprint that clarifies

- Who owns what

- How work flows through your organization
- Where accountability sits
- Where your operating model needs refinement

This becomes a foundational artifact for every AI initiative that follows. It reduces confusion, strengthens handoffs, and brings your entire AI ecosystem into focus.

Key Takeaways

You can think of the big takeaway from this chapter as a reminder that an AI operating model is really about people and how work gets done, not about chasing the newest tool. Ownership, accountability, roles, lifecycle, support, and platforms are not abstract concepts; they are the way you turn AI from a clever experiment into something the organization can rely on. When you know who owns a solution, who is accountable if it drifts, how ideas come in and move through the pipeline, where people go for help, and which platforms you are building on, you create a structure that lets people do their best work without guessing at every step. That is what turns AI from a side project into part of your organization's regular rhythm.

The other key learning is that your operating model is a living system, not a one-time diagram you check off in a workshop. As your AI projects mature, as vendors roll out new capabilities, and as your teams learn what works and what does not, the model should evolve with you. Over time, it becomes the blueprint that keeps you from reinventing the wheel with every new request and helps you scale from a handful of pilots to an enterprise-level program that feels intentional instead of accidental. That is the bridge into Chapter 10, where we will take this operating model and focus on what it really looks like to scale AI across the enterprise in a way that is sustainable, repeatable, and aligned to how your business runs.

CHAPTER 10

The Road Ahead: Scaling and Evolving Your AI Strategy

You do not rise to the level of your goals. You fall to the level of your systems.

—James Clear
Author of *Atomic Habits*

It's Not a Project, It's a Transformation

You have spent this book working through the IGNITE framework, and by now, it should be clear that it was never meant to be a one-and-done project checklist. IGNITE is a way to introduce AI into your organization in a responsible, repeatable, and grounded way that reflects how people actually work. You inspired people to care, gauged your readiness, nailed pilots that mattered, iterated your way through the mess, tracked impact, and built an operating model that can support real usage. All of that effort was about more than getting one agent into production. It was about proving to yourself and to your organization that AI can be part of your standard toolkit, not a side experiment in a single department.

J. Matfess, *Your New Colleague is a Copilot*, Inside Copilot,
https://doi.org/10.1007/979-8-8688-2619-1_10

This chapter is about what happens next. It is about scaling from that initial project or cluster of projects into something that touches the broader enterprise. We will talk about the prerequisites you need in place before you step on the gas, the patterns that show up when AI adoption starts to spread, and how to think about scale as a flywheel instead of a one-time rollout. We will look at the blockers that quietly stall progress and how to remove them, as well as the metrics you need to justify future investment and keep leadership engaged. In many ways, this is the capstone chapter. It takes everything you have learned so far and focuses it on a single question: how do you make this work not just once, but at real enterprise scale? Let's get started!

What "Scaling AI" Really Means

When we talk about scaling AI, it's not just about celebrating a couple of successful pilot projects and calling it a day. The real challenge (and the real opportunity) lies in creating a repeatable, sustainable approach. Scaling involves building muscle memory within your organization so that every new AI request doesn't feel like reinventing the wheel. You can and should look to other examples of technology scaling in your organization as a blueprint for how to scale AI.

Take, for example, a large property and casualty insurance firm I worked with almost ten years ago. Our story begins in the days of on-premises SharePoint 2010, when they were just dipping their toes into business process automation. Initially, IT had to own every project, from requirements gathering through production deployment. But as they scaled, they shifted from this IT-controlled process to empowering citizen developers across the business. They set up a center of excellence and a simple intake process. The idea was: you don't need IT to build everything for you, but IT should be in the loop. That way, when it came to disaster recovery or audit needs, they knew what was running where.

This consultative approach is an excellent parallel for scaling AI. It's about having a playbook and some best practices that make it easy to move from one successful AI proof of concept to the next without months of wheel-spinning. And that's the real key to scaling: repeatability and a kind of democratization of the tools. You could take a page from this company's playbook in planning to build the platform that AI solutions will run on. You can architect guardrails to encourage teams toward safe, but successful, outcomes, and you can also ensure cross-business sharing to accelerate disparate teams towards successful outcomes.

Now, culturally, the most significant shift is about embracing a mindset of experimentation. Much like we saw with the move to the cloud, it's not just about mastering new technical skills; it's about being willing to iterate using natural language and new interfaces. The user interface is no longer code; it's language. And that means people who are adaptable and ready to learn will naturally thrive. Those who resist may find themselves left behind not by AI itself, but by their peers who are making the most of it. But hopefully, you've begun to upskill your organization to be prepared for this change, as we discussed in Chapters 8, around AI literacy, and Chapter 9, regarding building your AI operating model. In the next section, we'll dive into the prerequisites you need before scaling AI.

Prerequisites: The Conditions You Must Have Before Scaling

Before you can scale AI in any meaningful way, you need stability. You cannot scale into chaos. If you try to accelerate before the foundation is ready, the organization will drown in inconsistent decisions, shadow tools, unclear ownership, and well-intentioned teams working at cross-purposes. Scaling only works when the groundwork has been laid with intention. These prerequisites act as the guardrails that keep the organization aligned as you move from isolated wins to an enterprise capability.

The first prerequisite is a clear AI operating model. You need to know who is responsible for what, how requests flow through the system, how decisions are made, and who is ultimately accountable. This is the connective tissue that keeps scattered AI work from becoming a liability. Without a defined structure, each new idea becomes a negotiation, and every new agent or automation becomes a small crisis. Chapter 9 walked through this in depth, because scaling is impossible until you have an operating model that people can trust.

You also need foundational AI literacy across your teams. This does not mean everyone becomes a prompt engineer. It means people understand what AI is good at, where it struggles, and how to interact with it responsibly. It means managers know how to guide their teams through the process. It means employees feel confident enough to adopt new tools rather than avoid them. Chapter 8 explored how literacy becomes the fuel that powers every stage of the Ignite framework. Without it, scaling turns into a bottleneck.

Next, you need early proof points from your pilots. These proof points are more than success stories. They demonstrate that the organization can navigate risk, that your data is ready enough, and that your approach to design and iteration produces results. They create the political capital that enables scaling. They are the evidence your leadership needs to say yes to broader investment. This connects directly to the work you did in Chapter 3, where pilots became your first meaningful tests of value.

A predictable iteration rhythm is another key condition. Iteration needs to feel normal and expected, not chaotic or reactive. Teams should know how feedback is gathered, how changes are prioritized, and how updates move through the system. When iteration becomes a muscle the organization uses regularly, scale becomes significantly easier. Chapter 4 covered this as part of the heart of your operating cadence.

Finally, you need baseline measurement and impact tracking. Scaling AI without measurement is like speeding down a highway at night with the headlights off. You need clarity on what matters, how you measure success, and how you communicate progress. These metrics guide investment, prevent drift, and help you avoid scaling things that do not work. Chapter 5 introduced this discipline, and at scale, it becomes even more critical.

Together, these prerequisites ensure that scaling is not just faster, but smarter. They create the environment where new solutions can be introduced with confidence, supported by structure, and aligned with a clear strategy. With these conditions in place, your organization is ready to take the next step toward enterprise-wide transformation.

The AI Adoption Flywheel

When you move beyond pilots and start thinking about enterprise-wide adoption, the goal is to create a flywheel. A flywheel is a system where progress reinforces itself. Each turn makes the next turn easier. Adoption stops being something you push and starts becoming something the organization naturally pulls toward.

In the context of AI, the flywheel has four major forces.

1. **More literacy leads to better ideas.**

   As teams build foundational AI literacy, they stop thinking in vague aspirations and start spotting real opportunities. They begin submitting higher-quality use cases, identifying better data sources, and shaping more grounded expectations. This raises the floor for every future request and helps inspire other groups about the potential business benefits of AI.

2. **Better ideas lead to stronger pilots.**

   The best pilots aren't random; they are strategic moves tied to business demand. Nailing these early projects gives you the momentum and internal buy-in to keep going. It's precisely what one of my P&C Insurance customers did: they turned their first few pilots into a foundation. By standardizing the forms and workflows early on, they paved the way for faster, more consistent rollouts down the road. It allowed them to scale through sharing lessons learned, celebrating successes, and transparency.

3. **Strong pilots produce proof points and champions.**

   Visible results change the entire conversation. You stop trying to convince leadership that AI is worth it, and they start asking how fast they can get it. As those early wins stack up, other teams will naturally want in. This is also when your internal champions reveal themselves. Pay close attention to the people driving this enthusiasm. Find them, support them, and use their success to fuel the next phase of growth. These "AI influencers" are going to help convince some of your most skeptical folks that this isn't just another fad and that there are benefits to be had.

4. **Champions and success stories create demand for more literacy.**

   Champions and success stories naturally fuel the demand for literacy. When someone gains recognition for a win, they rarely stop there; they look for the next opportunity to make an impact. These stories become the lifeblood of your internal marketing, from road shows to lunch-and-learns. Once people see their peers winning, they want to know how to do it too. The demand for access and training spikes, which drives literacy and feeds right back into the start of the cycle.

The flywheel begins to spin on its own. Every rotation picks up speed and becomes effortless. Eventually, the organization stops scaling AI because of a leadership mandate. It scales because the flywheel's momentum is impossible to stop.

BUILDING YOUR AI ADOPTION FLYWHEEL

To help you begin building your AI Adoption Flywheel, let's create a simple intranet site concept that serves as the home base for your AI Office or AI Center of Excellence. By the end of this exercise, you will have a clear outline of the pages, content, and even an assistant agent that can help people find AI policies, request help, and discover approved solutions.

What you will need:

- Paper or a whiteboard, or a simple drawing tool
- A note-taking app or document
- 45–60 minutes of focused time for you and maybe a few teammates to begin roughing out what this could look like.

Step 1: Define Who This Site Is For

Before you design anything, decide who your target audience is, and also ideally who you might want that audience to be.

1. Make a quick list of audiences that will visit this site. For example:
    - Business leaders
    - People managers

- Frontline staff
- IT and security teams
- Makers and power users

2. For each audience, write one sentence that starts with:
   - "When I visit the AI Office site, I want to..."
3. For example:
   - "When I visit the AI Office site, I want to know which AI tools are approved for my team."
   - "When I visit the AI Office site, I want to understand how to request a new AI pilot."
   - "When I visit the AI Office site, I want to know which tools or platforms we are currently evaluating."
   - "When I visit the AI Office site, I want to get help with building a new agent to support x-y-z use case."

These sentences will guide what content you need and how you organize it.

Step 2: Decide What Data You Need to Collect

The AI Office hub is not just a set of pages. It is also a place where you can collect information to help you govern and scale AI. Next, you'll create a simple list on your notepad or digital whiteboard with three columns:

- **Form or page**
- **Data you will collect**
- **How it will be used**

For example:

- **AI Idea or Use Case Intake Form**
    - **Data** – Requester's name, business unit, problem statement, data sources, data classification, expected impact
    - **Used For** – Prioritizing pilots, routing to the AI Office, tracking demand
- **AI Pilot Registry**
    - **Data** – Pilot name, owner, status, tools used, risk classification, start and end dates
    - **Used For** – Avoiding duplicate efforts, reporting to leadership, learning from prior work
- **AI Incident or Concern Form**
    - **Data** – What happened, system involved, data type, impact, who reported it
    - **Used For** – Improving guardrails, updating training, refining policies

Do not overcomplicate this. The goal is to make it very clear which forms and pages will give your AI Office the signal it needs to govern and support AI at an enterprise scale.

Step 3: Design the Information Architecture

Now translate the audience and data into a simple site structure.

On a blank page, draw

1. A **Home page** at the center
2. Branches from the Home page to four to six core sections. For example:
    - "Start Here" or "New to AI"
    - "Policies and Guardrails"
    - "Approved Tools and Use Cases"
    - "Request AI Help or a New Pilot"
    - "Training and AI Literacy"
    - "AI Office and Contacts"

Under each section, list two or three items you would surface right away. For example, under "Policies and Guardrails," you might list

- Plain language summary of AI policy
- Full legal policy document
- "What is allowed" and "What is not allowed" examples

Your goal is not a pixel-perfect design. You are creating a clear mental model of where people go and what they will find.

Step 4: Mock Up the Home Page

Next, leveraging the high-level information architecture that you just defined, create a rough mock-up of the actual Home page.

On a new page, draw

- A **top area** with
    - A short tagline for the AI Office
    - One sentence that explains what this site is for

- A **main content area** with tiles or cards for
  - "Start Here: How we use AI"
  - "Find AI Policies and Guardrails"
  - "See Approved AI Tools"
  - "Submit an AI Idea or Request"
  - "Training and Courses"
- A **right-hand or bottom area** with
  - "Recent announcements from the AI Office"
  - "Featured AI success story"

Label each element with a short description, such as "Button that links to intake form" or "Short 2-minute overview video."

This mock-up will serve as your blueprint for a real intranet page later.

Step 5: Design the "Ask the AI Office" Agent

Now bring an AI agent into the picture. This agent sits on your AI Office site and helps people navigate policies, procedures, and next steps.

Answer the following prompts:

1. **What is the agent's primary job?**

   Finish this sentence: "This agent exists to help employees..."

   Example: "This agent exists to help employees understand what is allowed, what is not allowed, and where to go next for AI support."

2. **What sources will it use?**

   List the content you want the agent to rely on:

   - AI policy and acceptable use guidelines
   - Data classification and sensitivity documentation

- AI Office intake process overview
- FAQ documents about AI tools and pilots

3. **What three questions should it answer very well?**

   Examples:

   - "Can I use this AI tool with customer data?"
   - "How do I request a new AI pilot for my team?"
   - "What training should I complete before using generative AI?"

4. **What should it never do?**

   Examples:

   - Never invent a new policy that does not exist
   - Never provide legal advice or handle sensitive information such as "social security numbers, credit card numbers, passports, etc."
   - Always link to the official policy page for anything sensitive

If you are using a platform like Copilot Studio or another agent builder, you can turn these answers into

- The agent description
- The list of knowledge sources to connect
- Guardrail instructions about tone, scope, and escalation

Step 6: Plan How People Will Discover and Use the Hub

Scaling only works if people know this hub exists and trust it; therefore, you will need to plan your communications when launching this new site. You will want to partner with folks from your Corporate Communications, Human Resources, and Change Management teams to identify the best channels to reach your co-workers.

Some questions that may help you identify the best channels to communicate through and challenges to address—not only to inform people that your site exists but also to keep them engaged—include the following:

- How will new employees learn about the AI Office site during onboarding?
- How will managers be prompted to send their teams here before starting new AI work?
- How will you keep the content fresh, so employees do not treat the site as "that old page that is never updated"?
- Does your company provide access to AI training platforms like LinkedIn Learning or Pluralsight that can be linked from your site?

From there, consider brainstorming two or three simple actions you can take, such as the following:

- Add the AI Office hub to onboarding checklists
- Ask leaders to reference the site in town halls when they talk about AI
- Publishing a news article on your Intranet

Step 7: Reflect

To close the exercise, write short answers to these questions:

- If you built this hub as sketched, what problem would it solve immediately?
- What is the minimal viable product that you could launch in the next 60 days?
- Which part of this design would give your AI Office the most leverage for scaling: the intake forms, the agent, or the training and policy pages?

These reflections become your starting backlog. They help you move from a sketch in a book to a real, scalable intranet presence that supports your employees' AI journey.

Your Scaling Architecture: Centralized, Federated, or Hybrid

As you look to scale AI development and innovation across your organization, one of the first choices you will make is how you want people to build and support solutions. This is really a decision about structure and control. Most organizations begin with one model and evolve into another as they mature. At a high level, here are the three approaches you can choose from:

Centralized - A single core team, often IT or a shared services group, owns all AI development. They build, deploy, and manage every solution.

Federated - A central IT function remains in place, but individual business units also have their own technical resources who can build or support AI solutions.

Hybrid - A mix of centralized and federated approaches. Some AI solutions stay under the core team, while others are built or maintained by business units based on risk, sensitivity, or complexity.

Most organizations start out centralized because it is the most controlled and predictable way to begin. I worked with a utility company that took this exact approach. Everything lived under IT. It kept things tightly governed, but it also limited creativity because no one outside of that team had the autonomy to try new ideas. You can move fast in a centralized model only when the central team has the capacity and the interest, and that becomes a bottleneck once demand starts to grow.

As organizations mature, many shift toward a federated model. This happens when the business is eager to experiment and has some technical talent of its own. I have seen this with one of my former clients where each business unit has a dedicated IT presence, even though there is still a global shared services group. This brings more speed and flexibility, but it can also create friction. Some platforms do not like highly distributed administration. People may end up with partial or inconsistent access. It is an improvement, but it comes with new complexities.

Over time, the most successful organizations end up in a hybrid model. They keep certain solutions under the central team because those projects involve sensitive data, have regulatory implications, or are simply too critical to distribute. At the same time, they empower the business to run with lower risk or department-specific projects once the right guardrails are in place. This is the sweet spot because it balances control with empowerment. It grows alongside your AI maturity and keeps the organization flexible without sacrificing trust or consistency.

Removing Blockers That Prevent Scale

The most significant barrier to scaling AI is rarely the technology itself. It is the people and how the organization perceives the work. Many companies make the mistake of treating AI as just another IT project that must be tightly controlled, but that mindset limits progress. As discussed in Chapter 9, scaling demands a genuine partnership between business and technology. Both sides must realize that AI cannot simply be bolted onto existing workflows. It reshapes roles, processes, and decision-making entirely. Without this mental shift, the initiative stalls before it ever has a chance to grow.

Then there is the chaos of unstructured data. Most early AI efforts start with simple agents connected to shared documents, but that data is often disorganized, mislabeled, and cluttered with outdated permissions. In the on-prem era, IT kept a tight grip on access. The move to the cloud gave business users the freedom to share and manage files independently, improving collaboration but introducing significant risk. To remove this blocker, you have to invest in hygiene. You need classification and organization to ensure the information feeding your AI is both reliable and safe.

We also see a recurring human blocker where business teams fail to recognize their role in the process. They often view AI as a product delivered to them rather than a capability they help enable. Overcoming this requires education and clear expectations. You may need to identify business champions to guide their peers, but the objective is not just creating more work. It is helping leaders understand that AI essentially exposes risks that were already there. It forces the organization to address them finally.

Finally, scale fails without a formal structure. AI must be treated as a legitimate program with visibility, resources, and accountability. A simple RACI model can clarify who is responsible, accountable, consulted, and informed.

Key Takeaways

Scaling AI is not an exercise in technology. It is an exercise in building the systems, habits, and mindsets that allow your organization to transform with confidence. Throughout this book, you have seen that successful AI adoption begins long before any model is deployed. It starts with inspiring people to care, understanding your readiness, selecting pilots that matter, and learning through structured iteration. It continues with tracking impact and building the operating model that gives your teams clarity and stability. These skills form the backbone of your AI practice. They create the conditions where AI becomes something the organization can depend on, not something it fears or avoids.

As you move forward, the most important lesson to carry with you is that AI grows where trust and structure already exist. Your role is to create the environment where people feel capable, supported, and excited to participate. When you combine literacy, guardrails, storytelling, and a clear system for scaling, you build the flywheel that keeps momentum alive. AI becomes less about individual projects and more about an ongoing transformation that helps your organization work smarter, move faster, and unlock new value. You now have the tools to guide that transformation. The next chapter of your AI journey begins with how you choose to put them into practice.

Index

A

J. Matfess, *Your New Colleague is a Copilot*, Inside Copilot,
https://doi.org/10.1007/979-8-8688-2619-1

B

C

D

E

F

G

H

I, J, K

L

M, N

O

P

U

V

W, X, Y, Z